Peter touches on some very intere
in his book *Doing Good by Doing G*
that many organisations are attem
and certainly have the right intent
few are executing their strategy to bring about the best return.
Peter's advice to the charity sector to step up and change their
ways, shifting from the old paradigm of just seeking donations,
is encouraging and if heeded will lead to a more engaged sector
and deeper relationship between corporate and charity. If you
are in business, part of a foundation or leading a charity, you
would be served well to read Peter's latest work.

— **Chris Cuffe,** Company Director, Investment
Professional and Philanthropist

Baines makes a highly practical contribution to how the best
businesses create value by having a more positive social impact.
And considering his track record of actually doing so, who
better to listen to.

— **Peter Sheahan**, author, founder and
CEO of ChangeLabs™

Peter Baines has correctly written that innovation and a sense of
the entrepreneurial spirit are the key to the future, irrespective
of industry or academic discipline. This is advice offered at an
important time in our collective search for best practices and
the truth.

— **William E. Strickland Jr**, President and CEO,
Manchester Bidwell Corporation

PETER BAINES

Founder of Hands Across the Water

DOING GOOD
by
DOING GOOD

WHY CREATING SHARED VALUE IS THE KEY TO
POWERING BUSINESS GROWTH AND INNOVATION

WILEY

Acknowledgements

In writing a book there are those who contribute to the text you hold in your hands right now and there are those who provide you with the love, inspiration, and at times space, to write. The contribution of both makes for what every author hopes is a quality reflection of their thinking.

Let me acknowledge the contribution of both groups.

Guy Downes is a genius. I first met Guy when from the back of the room he captured my one-hour keynote in a graphical representation, the likes of which I had never seen before. When it came time to write the book, Guy was the first person I contacted to be part of the project. His contribution throughout the book brings to it to life and you would have to agree he possesses a unique skill in what he does. I love the way his mind works and the benefit I see his corporate clients take from his work.

The book has a number of case studies and many of the contributors were most generous in their time and in sharing of their wisdom. Without their views and insights this book would be a reflection of my thoughts alone. It is the case studies, both of those contributing to the charity space and those working within, that add so much value. To each of these contributors who were so giving, please accept my deep appreciation.

The team at Wiley. The rise of self-publishing means that it really is within anyone's capacity to write a book. In such a crowded marketplace it then becomes even more important to get it right and surround yourself with a GREAT team. The entire team at

Wiley is that, a great team that kept me on-track, on-time and on-message. Thanks to Sarah, Lucy, Jem and Chris for staying with me during this process.

To the clients who I get to build these CSR programs with, thanks for the trust for believing there is another way of engaging with the community sector.

Now to the second group, those who provide the love, support and inspiration.

To each and every one of the Thai staff and the hundreds of Thai kids that I have had the pleasure of working with over the last decade, I continue to learn from you. I have become a nicer and more caring person just from spending time with you and seeing the way you live your lives no matter the challenges.

To the generous supporters of Hands who jump on a bike and ride across Thailand with me, or those who donate their hard earned money to us, you all confirm my belief there is another way of doing charity and people do want to do more than just give.

To my three beautiful children who I adore, you make me so incredibly proud in the decisions you make. Lachie, Kels and Jack, I love you guys not just because you are my kids, but because of the people you are. Some of my greatest moments over the last ten years are the ones we have spent together either in the snow or in the sun. I love you guys to bits.

Finally to Claire Thomas. I love what we create together and the lives we build each day. Your patience, not just during the writing of this book but in putting up with the crazy life I lead, is not found in everyone, but that's okay, I don't need everyone or anyone else for that matter, I have you. The love and support you give me CT makes this wild journey so much fun and I love you so deeply.

Preface

So how does a former police officer come to write a book on corporate social responsibility? I often ask myself the same question, as the path from where I began to where I am now has hardly been a predictable one.

After leaving school I soon found myself in uniform. I worked at Merrylands and Cabramatta police stations in the late eighties and early nineties. It was frustration over attending back-to-back domestic disputes rather than a passion for science that led me to join the Physical Evidence Section (later to become the Forensic Services Group) of the NSW Police. I found my place there and would spend the next 15 years 'on the tools', attending major crime scenes and incidents.

For 10 years I lived in rural New South Wales, where my three children, Lachlan, Kelsey and Jack were born. After years of driving up and down the New England and Newell highways investigating scenes of death and destruction, I was promoted to inspector and returned with my family to Sydney. When terrorism arrived on our doorstep with the Bali bombings in 2002, I was deployed as part of the Disaster Victim Identification (DVI) team. The work of the Australians in Bali cemented our important regional role in disaster response in Asia–Pacific.

Just over two years later, while on a family holiday at the beach on the south coast of New South Wales, I watched the 6 pm news lead with the tsunami that had just struck South-East Asia. Within days I returned to my DVI work, this time on a much larger scale, in Thailand. In what remains to this day the world's largest identification attempt undertaken following a disaster, 5395 bodies were recovered. I spent several months in Thailand, leading both the international and national teams in the disaster response. We faced unprecedented challenges that required unique solutions and strong leadership. I worked alongside some amazing people and had the opportunity to meet many individuals, both Thais and foreign visitors, who had lost family members.

But it was meeting the children who had lost their parents that would really change things for me. It was August, some eight months on from the tsunami, and there were 32 of them living in a tent, which was the only home they had. I couldn't change what had happened, but I felt it was within my power to change what happened next in their lives. This was the birth of the charity Hands Across the Water.

During the final two years of my career with NSW Police I worked on a counter-terrorism project with Interpol in Lyon, France, and with the United Nations Office on Drugs and Crime in South-East Asia.

I began raising money for Hands through paid speaking engagements, during which I talked about leadership. Pursuing the corporate speaking circuit and holding down a full-time job, while at the same time trying to build the charity, proved to be unsustainable over the longer term. I knew I could no longer do justice to all three and had to make a decision. At the end of 2008 I resigned from the police force after 22 years, putting my faith in my ability to draw an income from my speaking and my new consulting practice.

I have been fortunate enough to travel the globe speaking to audiences of all sizes, from all industries, and meeting some amazing people along the way. The more I spoke, the more Hands grew; as Hands grew, so did my corporate speaking, and I was able to turn what I learned into a successful consultancy.

Hands has grown to cover all points of the compass in Thailand. Several hundred children have found sanctuary in the seven centres we run across the country. At one centre we were able to halt the alarming mortality rate among children with

In the chapters that follow we will look at the following questions:

- What are the benefits to business of getting involved in community problems?
- If you're going to get involved, how do you select your partners?
- What are the options around getting involved, and how much involvement do you really want?
- Why does the concept of shared value make sense?
- How do you make your investment in the charity sector a profit centre?
- Why is it in everyone's interest that you're *doing good by doing good*?

Who should read this book?

I think there are five main groups of people who are going to take the most value out of reading this book:

- those with an interest in business who are looking for new opportunities to improve end-of-year returns

- those working within, or hoping to expand their knowledge of, corporate engagement
- those involved in the charity sector as charity leaders or directors on not-for-profit (NFP) boards
- those who call themselves philanthropists or who play a role in foundations that distribute money to charities and NFPs
- social entrepreneurs who love the excitement of building new business ventures while at the same time benefiting others.

In the following pages we'll explore how each of these groups stands to benefit from the case I'm going to make.

Essentially, the book represents my observation and interpretation of those who have worked within this space and have added immensely to their business or the company they work for and to their own personal wealth, and along the way have also managed to feed their soul. What ties them all together is that their pursuit of *doing good* has resulted in their *doing good*, and therein lies the magic.

The book contains a collection of case studies from public and private companies of various sizes who have adopted corporate social responsibility (CSR) in the past but have jumped ahead of the pack in developing a new style. In most cases they have changed the course of their giving in order to create a deeper impact in the communities they are working with, and consequently they have seen a direct improvement to their business. The improvement they have seen may take the form of raised morale, deeper engagement, a tighter workforce, new customers or increased brand awareness, and a number of these companies have already seen increases to their bottom line. But what you will see is that many of these results were incidental to and not the driving force behind their change in community engagement.

I should declare a personal interest in a number of the organisations I have profiled in this book, insofar as I have worked with them on a consulting basis to implement or overhaul their strategy for contribution and engagement with the community. There are also a number of case studies from companies whose presence or position I would love to take the credit for, but sadly I cannot. The entrepreneurial vision of Blake Mycoskie, the founder and 'Chief Shoe Giver' at TOMS, is an obvious choice. What I love most about the work of TOMS is the sheer simplicity that sees the model work so effectively. No messy formulas, no percentages from gross or net profits, just one for one. As a businessman Mycoskie has done very nicely from his social venture, and in my mind there is absolutely nothing wrong with that. The community can only benefit by encouraging and applauding those who, like Mycoskie, bring their skills and vision to this sector, rather than losing them to the corporate world.

Mycoskie doesn't have all the answers to the problems in developing countries; he doesn't pretend to. Is his model the only one to follow? Maybe not, but there are several million people in the developing world who, but for TOMS, would not have shoes on their feet today. And that has to be a good thing. Mycoskie was always going to be a huge success and make a stack of money, given his eye for opportunities and ability to turn concept into reality, and the children of Argentina, Nepal, Malawi, Kenya and Ethiopia are better off as a result of TOMS' commercial success.

If you have CSR attached to your job description, unless you are with quite a large organisation, there is a good chance this is not your only role. You may also be wearing a marketing or internal communications hat and CSR is just something the executive team thought should sit with you when they looked for a home for it on the org chart. Their thinking reflects how they see it: 'It's a nice thing to have in the organisation, but it's not sales, that's for sure. It's not operational. It's the softer side of things.' Even those of you who are working in a dedicated CSR role will probably have come from marketing, PR or internal comms. How does the fact that you work in marketing or communications qualify you to make the best decisions on something that can be so important to the business, and has so much potential if the resources are appropriately allocated?

You might rightly ask the same question of me. How does working in the forensic area investigating major crime for 20 years make me an authority on this? My answer is: the clear on who they want to support and on the projects they want to support. Many also require the provision of reports on how their money is spent. But very few look at the effectiveness of the charity or NFP or at how change to that organisation could see the better utilisation of many donors.

A case in point is the annual 'Failure Report' produced by the NGO Engineers Without Borders. The name of the organisation makes it clear what it does and where it works. This insightful report looks at what it has done (nothing new there) and also what *didn't* work. It then looks at the lessons to be learned and makes recommendations for next time. It's a wonderful, honest and courageous document and so refreshing to read.

An interesting report from Engineers Without Borders that speaks to this point concerned funding for the implementation of a water project in an underdeveloped area. The funding was to a Canadian group and was for the installation of a water system—specifically, a *new* system. While they were installing the water system, they were stepping over and removing the US-installed system that had broken down. The water would be drawn from the same source and delivered to the same community via very similar technology. The report found that for a fraction of the cost of the installation of the new system they could have made repairs to the US system that already serviced the community. They could not do that, however, because the funding conditions did not allow for maintenance or repairs but only for the installation of a new system. It didn't make sense to those on the ground and still doesn't make sense. It's a clear example of a donor determined to take sole credit and showing inflexibility in the use of their funds. It also shows where the power lies. Not equally between donor and NGO, not even close. My point is that if those at the foundation level choose to form a *partnership* rather than believing that because they have the money they should make all the decisions, the foundation's or donor's money could be more efficiently utilised.

The final group I see deriving real value from this book is the social entrepreneurs. These individuals may have worked in a dozen different jobs, following three or four different 'careers' by the age of 25, but haven't yet taken control of the company so have decided the best way to make their mark is to do it for themselves. The *socialpreneurs* are best described by T. E. Lawrence: 'All men dream: but not equally. Those who dream by night in the dusty recesses of their minds wake in the day to find that it was vanity: but the dreamers of the day are dangerous men, for they may act their dreams with open eyes, to make it possible'.

The socialpreneurs defiantly dream by day and more often than not they make it happen. They make it happen quickly, and if it doesn't come to fruition they move on and keep trying until it works. The best example in this book of a socialpreneur dreaming and making it happen, while epitomising the concept of *doing good by doing good*, is Blake Mycoskie, the founder of TOMS. He had kicked around a number of business ventures, some of which returned a nice profit, but they weren't feeding his soul so he walked away from them.

> '... The dreamers of the day are dangerous men, for they may act their dreams with open eyes, to make it possible.'

Actually he headed to Argentina to learn to play polo — and the rest, as they say, is history.

The socialpreneurs I've worked with don't need approval to make things happen. They don't conform to the limitations of funding through foundations or conditions attached to grants. They are driving a for-profit with a clear social benefit, and therein lies the magic; this is why it becomes sustainable and why they can set the course without the mindset limitations of those who believe they know what works best. When it is your money, rather than a gift or grant, a different level of freedom exists. I don't believe this is the only way forward, but it's one worth investing in and worth keeping an eye on. Plenty of them will fail, plenty will have dumb ideas, but among the coal there will be diamonds, and often those diamonds are worth a tonne.

I was part of a panel of judges at a humanitarian conference in the Philippines where we listened to presentations made by university students from places across Asia, including Nepal, Pakistan, India, Indonesia and many other countries. It was a bit like the reality TV show *The X Factor*, but for those with a social conscience. Just like the TV show there were plenty of auditions and pitches that never made it to the stage, and of those that did there were a few that were brilliant, and others that had the passion but were unlikely to crack the market, for now anyway. What was most inspiring about every one of the presentations was the desire, the lateral thinking and the headspace they were in. They had the courage and audacity to think they could tackle some huge social issues, and in some cases you knew they would.

So if you're in business looking to make a profit, working in the for-purpose space wanting to make a difference or you're a socialpreneur who wants to do both, fast, then together we can explore what works, what doesn't and what your best approach might be to *doing good by doing good*.

that is a desired outcome. By giving you have been seen to have 'done your bit', but by choosing just to give money you have limited your engagement and that might suit you.

Structured workplace giving programs are one of the simplest forms of giving. Companies like them because they are easy to implement, usually entailing little or no expense to them; the employees like them because they are pre-tax, set-and-forget donations; and the charities like them because it is often money for jam. But where is the engagement?

If you have no desire to divert resources away from core business and are more than happy to make an annual contribution, then you must accept the returns from that giving strategy will be limited also.

Is the issue, then, a lack of desire to create a more engaging experience or a lack of understanding of the opportunities that exist? I believe it is the latter. Australians constantly rank in the top 10 of donors on a per capita basis across the globe. But are we engaging in the most effective way of giving, and does the current model encourage growth?

The current model of most CSR programs, which is limited to one-off donations, matched grants and/or volunteering days, imposes an invisible ceiling on the sector, limiting potential and growth. Who then misses out? Well, everyone involved. The companies and individual donors don't capitalise on their donation and the charities aren't necessarily turning their donors into advocates and storytellers.

Missed opportunities

So where are the missed opportunities and why has it gone wrong when the intent to help is pure—or is it? In 'Beyond corporate social responsibility: Integrated external engagement', an article from McKinsey & Company (John Browne and Robin Nuttall, 'Beyond corporate social responsibility: Integrated external engagement' McKinsey & Company, www.mckinsey .com/insights, March 2013), authors John Browne and Robin Nuttall looked at the sector and came up with four serious flaws that are factors in CSR programs not working.

First, head office initiatives rarely gain the full support of the business and tend to break down in discussions over who pays and who gets the credit. The view outside of head office is that it is something they are often not consulted on; they haven't been involved in the selection process so why should they support it?

Second, centralised CSR teams can easily lose touch with reality and tend to take too narrow a view of the relevant external stakeholders. Managers on the ground have a much better understanding of the local context, who really matters and what can be delivered. Without that communication process across all levels of the company the initiative quickly comes to rest with a small head-office team who are often managing this on top of their normal functional responsibilities.

Third, CSR focuses too closely on limiting the downside. Companies often see it only as an exercise in protecting their reputations, allowing them to get away with irresponsible behaviour elsewhere. Effective external engagement is much more than that: it can attract new customers, motivate employees and build a better company.

Finally, CSR programs tend to be short-lived. Because they are separate from the commercial activity of a company, they survive on the whim of senior executives rather than on the value they deliver. These programs are therefore vulnerable when management changes or costs are cut.

The common thread in the four areas identified is the lack of any shared value. The CSR programs have been built for the wrong purpose and are run by the wrong people, and they are certainly not resourced as a normal business unit would be within the company.

In the past decade or so the mining industry has converted workplace safety, which used to be an add-on or even a hindrance, into a normal function that is evident in every part of the business. From senior management and site leaders through to contractors and site visitors, safety is at the forefront of how they operate. Why? Because it is good for business to be safe. The workers need to return home safely to their families after each shift. But the cost of workplace injuries also drove the change. So operating an unsafe workplace was no longer

Doing Good by Doing Good

acceptable. When something like safety is driven through every aspect of doing business, it is no longer a negotiable condition or something that's nice to have when business is going well; it is present regardless.

Within the mining industry they have been able to identify the costs of injuries in the course of business. Those costs may be related to loss of productivity, workplace investigations by regulators, fines imposed or union demands. Reducing injuries improves internal relationships between management and union bodies, creates an environment for better morale and increases productivity. No one doubts the commercial benefits—businesses that are safer will be more profitable.

CSR hasn't attracted the same type of leverage that safety has in the mining sector, in large part because of the inability to calculate the cost savings or gains from doing it well. It is often seen as sitting on the periphery of business and therefore it doesn't have the same advocates willing to drive it through the organisation. Unlike safety it is not mandated, regulated or enforced by legislation, and the reporting remains discretionary. For this reason the benefits to business need to be articulated and championed from the highest levels of the organisation.

A way forward

In addition to suggesting what is wrong with the current model, John Browne and Robin Nuttall, in the report 'Beyond Corporate Social Responsibility: Integrated external engagement', also propose a way forward. 'The logic is simple and compelling. The success of a business depends on its relationships with the external world—regulators, potential customers and staff, activists, and legislators. Decisions made at all levels of the business, from the boardroom to the shop floor, affect that relationship. For the business to be successful, decision making in every division and at every level must take account of those effects. External engagement cannot be separated from everyday business; it must be part and parcel of everyday business.'

The authors distinguished four key principles that applied across the various industries and companies with which they

Is there a better way?

worked: define what you contribute; know your stakeholders; apply world-class management; and engage radically.

Defining what you contribute doesn't mean changing your purpose for existence; it means determining clearly what you contribute to society. The greatest contribution is not in the end-of-year donation; it is in the overall benefit that is derived from the entity. 'It doesn't mean abandoning a focus on shareholder value; it means recognizing that you generate long-term value for shareholders only by delivering value to society as well.'

> The greatest contribution is not in the end-of-year donation; it is in the overall benefit that is derived from the entity.

The second key principle the authors found was in the value of knowing your stakeholders as well as you know your clients or customers. An in-depth knowledge of your partners means you are aware of trends and opportunities that might arise and build meaningful relationships.

In relation to the third and fourth principles, applying world-class management and engaging radically, the authors observe: 'A lot of companies start engagement too late. The natural temptation for many busy and cost-conscious executives is to delay acting until something hits them. That can be fatal'. Implementing change when it is not required and diverting resources from core business takes courage and tolerance by the board and the senior executive team, and buy-in from stakeholders. As the Chinese proverb goes, 'The best time to plant a tree was 20 years ago; the second best time is now'.

The authors conclude: 'A good relationship with NGOs, citizens, and governments is not some vague objective that's nice to achieve if possible. It is a key determinant of competitiveness, and companies need to start treating it as one. That does not mean they have to initiate philosophical inquiries into social responsibility and business ethics. But it does require them to recognize that traditional CSR fails the challenge by separating external engagement from everyday business. It also requires them to integrate external engagement deeply into every part of the business by defining what they contribute to society, knowing their stakeholders, engaging radically with them, and applying world-class management. In other words, it requires the same discipline that companies around the world apply to procurement, recruitment, strategy, and every other area of business. Those that have acted already are now reaping the rewards'.

Constraints on the charity sector

So if we accept the proposition that CSR in the form of corporate philanthropy will only ever produce limited returns, and we acknowledge that there are better ways of doing business, does that mean that the change required can or should be led by the corporate sector? What role does the charity, not-for-profit or for-purpose sector have in leading, or at the very least contributing to, the change? And do they have their own backyard in order, so as to make doing business on a more engaging level with corporate appealing?

Perhaps the problem is less to do with the business community not wanting to engage with the NFP sector and more to do with the business community acting with caution or trepidation when it comes to engaging with external partners with less control than they would have if they were part of the supply chain. If the NFP sector acted and performed more like business, would it make doing business with them more compelling?

In 2010 the Australian Productivity Commission released a report into the charity and not-for-profit sector in Australia. The report was the outcome of an extensive review of the entire sector and made recommendations addressing deficiencies and outlining directions for improvement. It posed a number of questions and made many observations that remain as relevant today as when the report was released.

Given how slow the charity and NFP sector is to move, it shouldn't be a surprise that many of the concerns identified in the report remain true today. The commission considered the nature of innovation and what is restraining those leading the organisations from adapting to changes and being progressive in their approach to fundraising and indeed problem solving. Chapter 9 of the commission's report 'Promoting Productivity and Social Innovation' made the following observations:

'Not-for-profit organisations (NFPs) face greater constraints on improving productivity than many for-profit businesses. These include difficulty in accessing funding for making investments in technology and training, lack of support for evaluation and planning, prescriptive service contracting by government, and in some cases resistance to change by volunteers, members and clients.'

Part of the reason for the lack of enthusiasm for embracing change and innovation can be attributed to the very sector itself, the returns to those working within and the expectations on performance. Many internal and external observers have the view that charities are doing a 'nice job' that is 'good' for the community.

There are a couple of views that prevail in society when you talk about the role that charity plays. The progressive view is that the future of charity rests with business, which will fill the gaps and lift up developing countries through social enterprise or shared value. They will be prepared to tackle the problems that exist locally and globally as they find ways in which to benefit commercially from the problems, which when viewed differently become opportunities. The theory Dan Pallotta promotes in his TED talk 'The way we think about charity is dead' supports business filling the gaps as those opportunities are realised, but he acknowledges that even then there will be at least 10 per cent for whom business and social enterprise will not provide the answers, and consequently there will always remain a role for charity as we know it.

The second and more mainstream view is to consider the NFPs as plugging the holes between government and corporate. I'm sure many consider the services as non-essential to the advancement of society as we know it. If we assume that attitude does exist, there is little wonder that NFPs don't feel the same pressure to adapt, improve and innovate as a commercial entity does.

If an NFP is supported by a group of volunteers, or a small paid (usually well below market value) workforce, at what point do they cease to be commercially viable? In the commercial marketplace success is measured by the return to investors and clearly their end-of-year success or otherwise is reported in a balance sheet; but what of the NFP? They will provide end-of-year reports showing their income versus expenditure, but if their income drops, or the gap between income and expenditure diminishes, the services they can offer just decrease. Shareholders seldom demand improvements and changes. Many of the 'shareholders' of the NFPs are silent recipients whose voice goes unheard by those calling the shots.

Without the commercial pressure to drive change and innovation within the NFP sector, where will it come from? Does the pressure to lead change rest with the leadership team and boards of these organisations? You would expect so, as they are the ones who set the direction and vision, and who drive operations towards achieving the goals set in the strategic plan. But where is *their* incentive to innovate and take risks? We know that if you want a risk-free organisation, if you want to eliminate mistakes, then perish the thought of innovating. Without risk there is no innovation. Speaking about risk in his book *Poke the Box*, Seth Godin observes, 'The cost of being wrong is less than the cost of doing nothing', but the NFP sector seldom rewards the risk takers.

In this sector it is deemed acceptable to pay less than true market value because 'we're a charity' (often said with slowly blinking eyes and a puppy-dog face). It is also considered wrong for the CEO of a large charity to be remunerated anywhere close to what they might be able to attract in the for-profit sector. So if you are not paying them appropriately in the first place you are highly unlikely to pay them bonuses or reward them for driving change or taking an innovative approach to business. What is bred, then, throughout the sector is the 'steady as she goes' approach, and when this is adopted those who were relevant run the risk of quickly becoming irrelevant, as social entrepreneurs step into this space and are prepared to lead with risk and innovation.

As the Productivity Commission report summarises the situation, 'NFPs' natural inclination to take innovative approaches to social problems is being restricted by the increasingly risk averse attitudes of funders and boards; limited resources; constraints on investments in knowledge; and reluctance to collaborate with other NFPs'.

Two different rule books

Dan Pallotta has a view on the charity sector, and a divisive one at that. He challenges the way charities operate, compensate their staff and market the good they do. The interesting thing on the division that he has created through his views is the debate within the charity sector, which can best be summed up as they either love him or hate him.

So what makes these views so divisive and how could they possibly contribute to creating a better relationship between the corporate and NFP sectors?

Firstly, what is he saying that is creating so much angst? If you were to sum it up in one word it would be *disparity*. He suggests that there are two different rule books; one for the for-profit sector and one for the not-for-profit sector. The disparity that exists presents itself in five main areas.

Compensation

Probably the second most contentious issue within the NFP sector, after the total amount that a charity spends on administration, is that of staff remuneration. If a charity CEO was paid an annual salary of $500 000 there would more than likely be an uprising and the CEO would be attacked as a parasite or worse. As Pallotta notes, however, the CEO of a company making violent video games earns $50 million a year and is put on the front cover of magazines as a success. Why, then, do we hold the view that someone who decides to devote their life to ending cancer in children, for example, shouldn't be equally well compensated? 'The model as it exists right now is you can do well for yourself and your family and be financially rewarded or you can do good for the NFP sector, but you can't do both.'

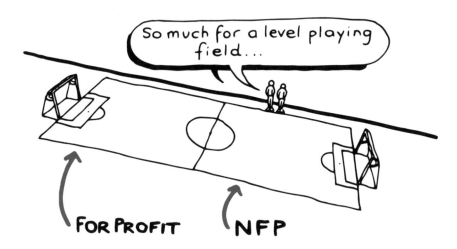

The best business minds that society produces graduate from university and head straight to the corporate sector to make their wealth. Twenty or thirty years after entering the corporate world they decide to leave and then look for a job that feeds their soul in the NFP sector. But the NFP has been handicapped by the fact that it has had to wait the 20 or 30 years for the smartest to accumulate the wealth to support their lifestyle, knowing it won't be coming in from the NFP sector, no matter what their skill base or the salary they can command in the corporate world.

Advertising and marketing

People don't want their donations spent on advertising or marketing; they want them spent on the needy. As the head of an international charity, I see this time and time again. The more mature donor will acknowledge that in running a multimillion-dollar business, which is what Hands Across the Water is, there will be expenses, and many will agree that to compete you need to spend part of your revenue on the running of the business. But ask them if their preference is for their donation to go into building a new home for at-risk children or to pay the salaries of administration staff working in Australia running the charity, and it is very clear where they want their money to go. The mature investor in charity will acknowledge the need to spend money, but they'd prefer it not be *their* money.

Is there a better way?

Dan Pallotta says that people are sick of being asked to donate money, which they see as being the least they can do. He says that people want to be asked to contribute in more meaningful ways to the causes they feel passionately about. Pallotta created long-distance bike rides and walks for charity. In a nine-year period more than 182 000 people participated. They were able to reach these numbers through advertising and marketing, by spending the charity's funds to grow the participation rates. They used the funds to buy full-page ads in *The New York Times*, *The Boston Globe* and advertise on primetime TV and radio.

Pallotta points out that giving in the US has remained consistent at 2 per cent over the past 40 years, which indicates that the NFP sector has not been able to wrest any of that spending from the for-profit area. Whether you agree or disagree with his views, he mounts a challenging argument that something needs to be done differently, because we can't continue to do the same thing and hope for a different outcome.

Tolerance of risk

The debate within the NFP sector when it comes to measuring effectiveness is over what constitutes a suitable measure. There is a strong voice that dollars spent on administration shouldn't be used as a measure. A regular (absurd, I would suggest) comment is that those spending low or no amounts on admin are home to scams or are grossly ineffective. These voices, I would suggest, hail from charities that aren't too happy with their level of spend or accountability and therefore want to disregard that measure. They propose that another useful measure might be the effectiveness of the charities. This sounds reasonable, and I have a director on the Hands board who often challenges us by saying, 'It's great that we don't spend donors' money on administration, but the equally important question is "are we spending donors' money in the most effective and efficient ways?".'

Is there a risk in measuring effectiveness of the charity? Well, it depends whether you measure it over the life of an individual campaign or in relation to the impact that you have on an annual basis. The risk when you start measuring on success or failure is you breed a culture that becomes intolerant of risk, and risk intolerance kills innovation. The NFP sector *cannot* survive without the opportunity to innovate. It is through innovation that the solution to many of the challenges the NFP exists to address will be found.

> The NFP sector *cannot* survive without the opportunity to innovate. It is through innovation that the solution to many of the challenges the NFP exists to address will be found.

Time

In talking about the time afforded to business, Pallotta cites the example of Amazon, which took six years before it turned a profit. Imagine if a charity were to take the first six years of fundraising to build its base *before* helping any of those in need. Such a position would not be tolerated and indeed would likely be illegal; at the very least it would be difficult to imagine the funding for such a model continuing beyond a year or so. Building Hands Across the Water, the greatest change to the income that flowed into the charity was on the back of the completion of the first home. Credibility runs parallel to success in the charity space. The more you are doing the more you are likely to receive, which allows you to continue to do more.

Currently the NFP sector faces the problem of an inability to attract people into the sector at equal compensation levels. Those working within the sector don't have the freedom to compete for market share by advertising or marketing, and there is a low tolerance for risks or mistakes, which hampers innovation. With anything that is done, results need to be produced pretty quickly as we don't have the time afforded to those in the for-profit space.

Capital

The for-profit sector can raise additional capital by selling shares in the business, which allows the business to grow, acquire or invest in new infrastructure. They have the ability to use their profits in various ways. The only source of capital open to the NFP sector is raising donations.

A need for balance

If we want to change the face of charity and increase the services we are offering, three real options exist:

1   We drive overheads down within the NFP sector by reducing the spend on salaries, advertising and administration. We ask the CEOs to take home less, even though we accept they are paid well below what for-profit CEOs can command.

2   We spend more in the NFP sector to drive growth. Our ultimate aim is that donors, through successful marketing and advertising campaigns, and even a shift in consciousness, increase their giving, which provides us with more to spend on social services.

3   We create opportunities for social entrepreneurs through the concept of *doing good by doing good*.

The first of the three options is flawed and unsustainable if we want to see any real growth. It flies in the face of most of the informed commentators in this space, from the thoughtful Dan Pallotta through to the authors of the Productivity Commission report and those in between. Innovation, leadership and growth within the NFP space requires investment, which will allow competition and 'air time' with the for-profit space.

Increasing the level of giving will generate a larger pie and greater access, but giving alone is not the answer either. The creation of shared experiences will enable people to be involved, to feed that part of their soul that currently goes hungry.

The third option, of creating more shared value between business and charity, goes to the heart of allowing people to satisfy their need to do well and build a good life for themselves while also allowing for the community around them to prosper. This model does not rely only on the generosity of the giver. Power does not sit with one side alone; it is shared. This creation of mutual dependence ensures that each side has an interest in the continuing growth of the other.

The question that then emerges is how do you create enough value for people to cross the road to do business with you as opposed to one of the hundreds of others like you?

You don't have to agree that Dan Pallotta's way forward is the right one. He has had successes and failures but there is merit in a number of his propositions. Perhaps his strategies are really best suited to very large charities. But it is hard to argue with the facts around the limitations that exist within the NFP sector when competing with the for-profit sector.

So when we suggest business should consider changing the way they engage with the NFP sector or work towards a model that more closely represents shared value or conscious capitalism, perhaps we should also be suggesting the charity sector make some fundamental changes if we want a different type of relationship.

As a footnote to this discussion on the charity sector, as chairman of Hands Across the Water I have a self-interest. In this chapter I have advocated appropriate remuneration of NFP staff, and I support the freedom of charities to commit appropriate resources to marketing, advertising and, importantly, to the development of its staff. I firmly believe that there is a need for balance to create a more level playing field between the FP and NFP sectors. But these views are not in support of my personal position. As the founder and chairman of Hands Across the Water, I receive no payment for the time I allocate to the charity. I cover all my own personal expenses and the charity operates from a position that 100 per cent of all donations go to the children and projects we run in Thailand. Not one cent of donors' money is spent on administration or fundraising. The model on which Hands was created makes it possible to operate under these principles.

- CSR can be briefly defined as 'how companies undertake their activities to have a positive impact upon society'.

- The view of CSR is expanding to include the broader concepts of *shared value* and *conscious capitalism*.

- Shared value is the outcome when business creates both economic value and value for society by addressing community needs and challenges. Shared value is not about cause marketing or programs such as employee giving, employee volunteering or matched giving programs. It looks for opportunities within new markets that address a community need, incorporating the entire value chain into the process along with the concept of local cluster development.

- In the words of Mackey and Sisodia, companies that embrace conscious capitalism 'create positive impacts for customers, employees, suppliers, communities and the environment, resulting in exceptional customer experiences, less turnover, lower overhead costs, higher profits, and sustained growth'.

- Two distinct rulebooks exist—one for the for-profit and one for the not-for-profit. The NFP is held back by its inability to match the FP in the areas of compensation for leaders, advertising and marketing, tolerance of risk, time and use of capital.

chapter 2

HOW TO
ENGAGE

The decision has been made: you are going to start giving back and you want to engage with a not-for-profit. There are some rules to engaging with the sector, and to start with we need to learn some of the language. Those working in the sector prefer that you talk about 'contributing' rather than 'giving back' and many like to be known as the 'for-purpose' sector as opposed to the 'not-for-profit' sector. As Ronni Kahn, the founder of OzHarvest, puts it, 'the business sector doesn't call itself the "we don't make a loss sector" so why should we be defined by what we don't do?'.

The next thing is that if those looking to enter the for-purpose sector possess the mindset that they are part of a hugely successful business and therefore have the answers for a charity, that might not work too well either.

Entering the for-purpose sector

I was recently part of a leadership development program that was aimed at executives who were looking to exit the corporate world either completely or in part and head for an executive or board position in the for-purpose sector. Each had enjoyed significant success in the corporate world and they shared a passion to contribute to the for-purpose space. And it was clear they weren't doing it to enhance their CV or to make themselves more attractive as a corporate citizen or prospect. From my read of the room they were doing it because they really wanted to spend time feeding their soul. One described himself as a 'reformed lawyer' now looking to engage in a more meaningful pursuit—his description, not mine.

It wasn't the success they had enjoyed that surprised me; neither was it their desire to seek fulfilment in another way. These are the people I meet on a weekly basis after I speak at conferences. They want to understand how they can produce what I have created with Hands—not necessarily to build their own charity, but to find reward and meaning in something outside of their current lives. They are a different group from those who come up wanting to volunteer and spend time with the kids. They have a much sharper and more well-defined vision of what they want.

What did surprise me listening to their journey was the difficulty many of these highly successful individuals were having in securing a spot of significance in the for-purpose space. For many of them the challenge had been much harder than they had anticipated. The message that was coming back from the sector was, 'You undoubtedly have great skills, but we want to know you are committed to our sector'; or, in the words of Michael Trail, the CEO of Social Ventures Australia, 'We don't care what you know, until we know that you care'.

Whether it is an individual or a company looking to enter the for-purpose space, there are similarities in the approach.

Consider why

What is the motivation for entering the sector? Here some honest conversations are needed. Is it a marketing exercise for the business? If it is to build a presence to offset profit or potential poor performance in another area, that needs to be put on the table. If an individual is looking to gain a position on the charity board to

> Without the clarity on why, finding the right fit may prove difficult.

improve their chances of obtaining a paid position on a commercial board in the future, that too needs to be honestly discussed.

Without the clarity gained from answering the why question, the only way their needs will be met is by accident. If an individual is looking at a place on a charity board as a stepping stone, there will be opportunities that allow for that in a start-up charity that can't offer the compensation that an established charity can. The emerging director may find that the greatest impact they can make in a short period of time, thus meeting their needs, is with such a start-up. Without the clarity on why, finding the right fit may prove difficult.

Define the strategy

Once the question why has been answered, then it becomes possible to build a strategy and allow a team to move forward to execute it. In chapter 12 I look at the decision-making process you might go through in aligning yourself with the right charity partner. Whether as a director or executive or as a corporate charity partner, defining your guiding principles will allow you to filter who it is you want to work with.

Among the biggest things to get right and invest the time in are the two Cs of culture and capacity. These are important considerations from both sides of the equation. The charity that is supporting the rights of women and children in developing countries doesn't want to find that its business partner, through a third party relationship, is involved in the use of child labour in the manufacture of a component it is selling. In the same way, the business doesn't want to find that the charity they thought was selling the dream of clean water for all is syphoning off 80 per cent of its revenue to support a religious agenda. There's nothing wrong with pursuing one's religion, but the business partner should have clarity around that and be able to make an informed decision. It's about full disclosure and ensuring there is a *cultural* fit between all parties, and for that due diligence is required.

The second C to get clear on is *capacity*. Many decisions made around charity are based on emotion. A desire to 'feed the soul' or 'make a difference' lies behind the compulsion to act. I have witnessed many organisations and individuals make commitments based on emotion rather than logic. However, once the emotion is gone, or at the very least is tempered by time and experience, then the capacity they imagined they had to give shrinks. That capacity may be on an organisational level around money or resources or on an individual level around time. Beware of the new volunteer who promises you the world, because often their capacity doesn't go anywhere near matching their intent.

Doing Good by Doing Good

Consider your give

In most cases, what you bring to the table as a business partner and what you could *potentially* bring to the table are two very different things. Often it starts out with a contribution of money, and as the relationship progresses over time, the opportunity to give more but in different currencies emerges. If we can clarify the potential and realise the true value of what we bring to the table, the relationship can profit from the very beginning.

It's not just about the money, and sometimes it's not about the money at all. The case study of the Sheraton Grande Sukhumvit in Bangkok offers a classic example of a company that built a unique offering for their clients that allowed them to give via the hotel to those in need. No money was exchanged between any of the parties involved, yet it remains one of the best programs I have built for a corporate.

> If we can clarify the potential and realise the true value of what we bring to the table, the relationship can profit from the very beginning.

Case study: Sheraton Grande Sukhumvit

As a keynote speaker I get to live this pretty cool life of quite literally travelling the globe speaking to the widest range of audiences you can imagine. One week I will be speaking to coal-miners in outback Queensland, the next to doctors in Spain followed by hairdressers in Phuket. Whatever the case, I have found that one thing happens, not every time I speak, but more frequently than not. You see, often I will be speaking about how I built Hands into what it is today. Depending on the desired outcomes of the client, the lessons may be framed around pursuing your dreams, focusing on results and not excuses, or having the courage to make the really tough decisions in life. After I've finished speaking I'll chat with those who want to say hello and then while I'm packing up I'll be approached by someone who fits the following demographic.

They will be in their mid forties, will hold a senior position in the area in which they work and will usually be financially secure. Children, if they have them, will either be in their later years of school or have finished school. Work, while challenging and demanding and usually involving long hours, no longer provides the stimulation it once did and they find something is missing in their lives. It's not related to possessions or income or securing the next promotion. The lack is at a deeper level, at the level of their soul, and this is what has been prodded during my keynote.

I share the stories of building a multimillion-dollar charity from the ground up and enjoying the rewards of seeing the change in the lives of those who engage with us. I can give the names of the kids who, but for Hands, wouldn't be alive today. I talk about the experience of working with kids with HIV and seeing their tiny bodies transformed as they grow in strength from the food and medicines we are able to provide, and it's these very real and meaningful experiences that challenge those in the audience who have been waiting for a light to be shone on them. They have earned the big dollars, they have enjoyed the trappings of the good life, but it's a while since their soul has been nourished in the work they do.

The stories of making a difference, seeing the change in lives, particularly among the vulnerable of our society, the children who have been abused, sold or left for dead … Now here's an opportunity for them to nourish their soul and make the difference they have longed for. I see it in their eyes. I hear it in their tone of voice. They don't come to me with the confidence of having the answers; they come with respect, having just acknowledged to themselves that their life is not as complete as many sitting around them would have thought. They understand that the pair of BMWs in the driveway at home hasn't addressed the lack, and until now they didn't know what would.

It's a conversation they want to have, but it's one they want to have in private. Would they find it embarrassing to acknowledge to those they work with that the thrill of the chase or the next deal is no longer driving and stimulating them? I'm not sure, but it's the conversation, spoken quietly, of 'I want to do what you do'. There's no need for clarification. They are not talking about travelling the world speaking, and they're not talking about leading bike tours. They are talking about doing *something* to feed their soul.

It was when I was speaking with Richard Chapman, the general manager of one of the finest hotels in Thailand, the Sheraton Grande in Sukhumvit, that this group came to mind and I finally knew how I could create opportunities for them. The Sheraton Grande is a business hotel and my relationship with Richard started when he invited me to speak at the annual meeting of the general managers for Indochina. Part of my brief was to speak to them on leadership and CSR, with a request attached that I put forward any ideas I might have on how the hotel could better contribute to the community in which they live and operate.

The hotel is located in the business area of Sukhumvit and therefore caters mainly to business travellers. It is a five-star hotel whose guests are not looking for a budget experience but are generally more senior business travellers. Richard explained to me that the hotel raised funds towards their annual contribution to UNICEF through the equivalent of a one-dollar donation attached to each guest's bill. The UNICEF contribution is not insignificant by any measure, especially since all the properties within the Sheraton Group participate. My conversation with Richard went something like this:

PB: How do you think the guest feels knowing they have contributed one dollar to charity?

RC: I don't think they would feel very much at all.

PB: Do you think many of them would even notice this on the bill?

RC: They might notice, but I don't think it's a major consideration for them.

PB: In fact, many of your guests would be travelling on a corporate card so the contribution is not theirs but that of the company they represent.

RC: Correct.

PB: So you would agree there is very little attachment to the dollar added to the bill?

RC: I would agree.

PB: Do you think it changes the experience of your staff who are processing the donation? Do they feel good about it?

RC: No, I wouldn't think it changes the experience for them in any real way.

PB: Do any of the local charities or those in need in Sukhumvit or indeed Bangkok benefit from this transaction?

RC: No, not to my knowledge.

PB: Are you aware of any change to those in need that this brings about?

RC: Not directly, no.

PB: There's no doubt that the totality of this exercise through the collection of funds across the entire group allows massive change to be achieved, I don't underestimate that.

RC: Yes, I agree. Since the Sheraton Group first adopted this practice we have donated more than US$30 million to UNICEF via the Check Out for Children program.

PB: That surely is a staggering amount of money and is evidence of how a little can mean a lot. But as an experience or engagement strategy I think it is fair to say that the hotel guests don't benefit, and your staff and the local community aren't really benefiting either.

RC: I agree.

I then had Richard profile his most frequent guests for me so I could understand who was staying at his hotel and how often they stayed (please note that no personal data that would allow me to identify these guests was disclosed). What he told me was that these guests were staying two nights on average 10 to 12 times a year. What was more interesting, as he described the typical business guest, was that it became very clear to me they exactly fit the profile of those who were approaching me at the end of my keynotes.

Then it became very simple and clear: all he needed to do was find those guests who fit into both categories and then create the opportunity that many of them were looking for. Having profiled those hotel guests who, given the opportunity, would jump at the chance to do something that would 'feed their soul', it was then time to find those living, working or studying in the local area who would benefit from support and mentoring. Not too surprisingly, that was relatively easy to do.

In a simple form we were building a mentoring program between those with the knowledge and those who could benefit from that knowledge and without such a program would never be likely to access the wisdom that resides in their mentors. The mentoring program looks at the development around core skills such as building strong relationships with partners, strategic planning, fundraising, building governance, and developing processes and systems.

So how do the hotel, Richard and his staff benefit from this?

Knowing them as he does, Richard selected from among his guests those he would invite to be part of the program. Many who were staying at the hotel for two nights had a pretty full agenda so would need to add a night onto their trip to accommodate the program. By stepping into the program, they are increasing their spend at the hotel by 50 per cent per stay. But that is just the start of the benefits to the hotel, outside of the good that is done through the mentoring.

Let's look at the return the hotel gained from running this program:

- The guests who were invited to be part of the program increased their 'nights per stay' by 50 per cent.

- Their in-house dining spend rose by an equivalent of 50 per cent per stay.

- New business customers were attracted to the hotel based on this program alone. How did that happen? The vast majority of program participants are international guests who are flying to Thailand for business. We have already profiled them as mainly successful executives holding senior positions within their business. They are staying at a five-star hotel and are naturally flying business class at a minimum. On their flight to Thailand they will of course get to talking to the passenger sitting next to them, and the topic of conversation will turn very quickly to their reason for visiting Bangkok. After a rundown on the business side our participants then speak with excitement of the difference they are making to the lives of those they have been supporting and mentoring over the past several months and how rewarding they are finding it. Intrigued, the passenger seated next to them expresses a desire to be part of the program, whereupon our mentor then mentions that to be eligible they would need to be staying at the Sheraton Grande in Sukhumvit. Next thing you know the Sheraton Grande has secured the patronage of a new high-value guest.

- The brand image of the hotel improves as it is seen as a valued member of the community through this program that is benefiting so many within the local area.

- The new program allows the hotel to start talking internally and then externally about what they are doing and the success they are having. It creates a new dialogue that was previously confined to hotel services, discounts or promotions. Now there is an additional reason to reach out and their communication is taken to a new level.

- The staff of the hotel are highly trained and customer service is at the core of what they do, but they are in the service industry and encounter some demanding clients. This new program brings a heightened level of engagement to their work as they see the benefits to their community and they are part of the change being created.

- The customer retention rate is a concern for everyone in business. In addition to attracting new business you want to retain the established relationships you have. The program not only increased the retention rate of those undertaking the program, but anecdotal evidence suggests those guests who were not part of the program, but were aware of it, were impressed and saw it as another reason to remain loyal to the hotel.

- Create a loyalty program or club that is hard to get into and you create demand. The very nature of the exclusiveness of the mentor club within the hotel started to drive interest in the program from those who saw it as something they should be part of.

The program is successful because it is built on experiences and only works when there is engagement. When you create meaningful experiences, you build engagement followed by commitment. The program was driven by the general manager at a time when political unrest within the country meant occupancy rates were low. The idea grew out of his desire, not to create new business, but to make a valuable contribution to the community.

There aren't too many ROI metrics for a CSR program that are not met within the Sheraton example, but no money changes hands. All of this has been achieved by creating shared experiences, which has led to a deep level of engagement not previously known within the hotel.

The Sheraton Grande mentoring program serves as an example of the types of investment that can be made within the social sector when there is a real desire, commitment and willingness to go beyond what everyone else is doing in just donating money.

Part of the program's magic lies in its simplicity and the fact that it didn't rely on the usual injection of money from the corporate to the charity partner. It challenges the mindset of what CSR is and is a great example of the concept of shared value. It's what *doing good by doing good* is all about.

> When you create meaningful experiences, you build engagement followed by commitment.

Channels of engagement

So what are the typical ways a corporate can look to engage with the for-purpose sector?

Donations

The lifeblood of all charities is money. Donations can take a number of different forms. The easiest transaction is the large one-off donation that involves little more than the shaking of hands and sharing of cake at a cheque-handover ceremony in front of the corporate logo. But although they may be transactionally the simplest, they are also likely to be the least engaging for all involved. When a member of the leadership team hands over a cheque that represents a portion of that company's net profits, who feels good about it and who gets to share in the experience? There will be a photo in the company newsletter or on the intranet, but few get to share directly in the experience; and if the money has come from company profits few in the business will really care.

If the donation is the result of matched dollar-for-dollar programs in which the staff contribute money and the company matches those donations, then the level of engagement will increase somewhat as the staff have some skin in the game and consequently become interested to some degree.

Workplace giving

This takes the form of salary deductions, with small amounts deducted from the employee according to the frequency of their pay cycle—weekly, fortnightly or monthly. Usually it is a scheme that the employee will sign up to when they join the organisation and are going through induction. For example, they will be handed their security pass, locker key, social club deduction form and workplace giving form. The employee will often sign the form (because who wants to be seen as a tight-arse on their first day?) without any real connection to the charity they have just signed up to support.

This form of fundraising is a bit like the dollar that is added to the bill when you check out of the hotel. Not a lot of emotional attachment and little opportunity to understand where the money is going or the difference it is making. Such a scheme is most valuable when the company is large and the dollars are spread over a small number of charities. Significant money can certainly be raised, but it requires the numbers for efficiency. The flip side of the benefits from larger organisations and larger funds raised is that the message becomes more generic and it's harder to reach everyone or for them to feel as though they are really making a difference. The thing to remember is they might be small drops in the ocean, but the ocean is made up of lots of small drops.

Fundraising events

This is where we start to move towards a more engaged model and to introduce the experiences. The types of events that can be held to raise money for the charity of choice really are limited only by imagination and desire. They can be small business units within large organisations, or the entire company may choose to get on board. Here are some examples of how easy it is to contribute and bring an experience into the workplace:

- Red Nose Day was one of the first campaigns to invite the general public to get on board. Held annually on the last Friday in June, it is the major fundraiser for SIDS and Kids. Funds raised through Red Nose Day activities assist the charity in providing vital services and programs to the Australian community. SIDS and Kids is dedicated to saving the lives of babies and children during pregnancy, birth, infancy and childhood, and to supporting bereaved families.

- Jeans for Genes Day is a national day when people wear jeans and contribute funds for research into birth defects and diseases such as cancer, epilepsy and a range of genetic disorders. On the first Friday in August each year workplaces, schools and streets become a sea of denim. Money raised on the day helps scientists at the Children's Medical Research Institute discover treatments and cures for childhood disease.

- The Leukaemia Foundation World's Greatest Shave invites everyone to shave or colour their hair for a good cause. The campaign raises about half the money the Leukaemia Foundation needs to fund its important research work and support of people with blood cancer.

- Australia's Biggest Morning Tea is an initiative that invites people to come together for morning tea during the months of May and June to raise money for cancer research. It's an easy one for business groups to pull off, because who doesn't stop for a cup of tea a couple of times a day? And if you don't, it's a great reason to start.

These four national events are examples of really low-effort interaction. Open to all without any barriers based on age, fitness, race or religion, they have been designed as campaigns that will have the greatest reach. The morning tea campaign run by the Cancer Council stretches over two months! Red Nose Day had massive participation in the early years, but here as elsewhere members of the public have shown they will move their support based not on the worth of the cause, but on the level of interaction and engagement they personally experience.

Each of the initiatives invites a team, work unit or business to contribute, and each is aimed at raising awareness of the issue in addition to money. In terms of engagement, the value of these days is greater than the workplace-giving model because they bring people together to share an experience and give them something new to talk about. The fundraising component will be limited to the time around the event.

For organisations looking to step the experience up a notch there are opportunities to take on something bigger, whether in the scale of the event, the fundraising attached to the event, or the level of involvement. Single-day events and multi-day events are increasingly popular. The multi-day events require a much greater level of commitment; in the main they are exclusionary based on ability or fitness, but they raise thousands more per entrant and the level of experience can be massive.

A wide variety of entry-level walks, runs, swims and rides take place across the country throughout the year, offering endless opportunities as fundraising events.

- The MS Society started the Sydney to the Gong Bike Ride 33 years ago, inviting people to ride from Sydney to Wollongong in aid of research and support for those suffering from multiple sclerosis. There are now two rides run in conjunction with each other, offering 55 km and 85 km alternatives.

- The Ride to Conquer Cancer, a two-day, 200 km ride held in Sydney, Brisbane, Melbourne and Perth, steps up the commitment and entry level for riders above that of the Gong Ride. Each ride supports a medical facility or research centre in their respective state.

- Oxfam Trailwalker is an event held across the country in which teams of four walk 100 kilometres through bushland in 48 hours. Each team is required to raise a minimum of $1400. The number of teams ranges from 800 in Melbourne to 550 in Sydney, 450 in Perth and 400 in Brisbane. The events, which sell out each year, require a huge level of commitment and physical endurance.

The increasing popularity of bike riding has seen the rise of long-distance bike rides such as the Tour de Cure, Chain Reaction and Hands Across the Water rides.

- The Hands ride covers 800 kilometres in eight days with a minimum fundraising entry level of $10 000 per ride. It is a very different ride from the Tour de Cure or the Chain Reaction ride, offering entry to those who are not accomplished riders. I like to call it a tour with a challenge. The Hands ride offers sufficient challenge to appeal to those who ride often but is achievable by those who are just returning to cycling, many for the first time since they got their driver's licence.

- The Chain Reaction ride is billed as the 'Ultimate Corporate Bike Challenge'. It is not a mass participation event and individuals can't sign up on their own. There is a significant buy-in cost for the teams, who ride 1000 kilometres over seven days.

- The Tour de Cure ride is based on a similar model, covering a similar distance, with $10 000 per ride minimum fundraising, but it is open to individual riders.

As the entry level rises for these events, so too does the levels of experience, engagement and funds raised. The harder they are to participate in, the more exclusive they become. Chain Reaction relies on strict entry criteria as a drawcard to corporates who see the advantage of this model.

What is interesting, though, is when you start to consider the funds raised per campaign. When you look at similar-sized organisations, output in running the events and reach, there isn't a lot of difference. For an event such as Australia's Biggest Morning Tea, huge numbers participate across Australia, exceeding 35000 during the last tea-break; and more than $12 million is raised. Break that down to state level and it is comparable to the money raised by the state rides conducted by Chain Reaction, but they will have about forty riders on the road.

Figure 2.1 shows the correlation between the number of participants and the entry requirements against the money raised per campaign. The higher the number of participants, the lower the entry requirements. Jeans for Genes Day and Australia's Biggest Morning Tea have very high participation rates with little to no entry criteria. Conversely, the Hands and Chain Reaction rides have very high entry requirements and low participation rates. But across the various campaigns there is not a major differentiation between the dollars raised.

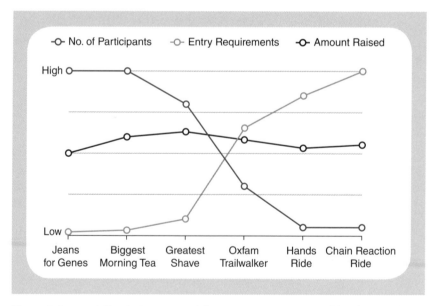

Figure 2.1: correlation between participants, engagement and funds raised

From an engagement point of view, forgetting for a minute the money raised, which campaign is more likely to bring benefits to the business—the morning tea, which will touch many over a very short period of time, or the rides, which touch a few in a deeply engaging way? The morning tea reaches far more people but their experience is short-lived and, it's probably fair to say, not life-changing for those participating. The long-distance bike rides take a 12-month commitment by the riders in fundraising, training and time. Many of them will achieve 'firsts' during the ride. They will be fitter and healthier for the experience and you can't participate in such a gruelling, week-long event and not be changed. But the change, although very deep for each rider, is restricted in large part to the riders.

As to which is likely to bring more benefits to the business, each campaign has its place in helping the corporate engage with the community and their charity partners. Each will appeal to a very different market, and all these considerations must be taken into account when planning the strategy for engagement. What is clear is that when it comes to involvement there is an option to suit *everyone*.

If corporate donations, or corporate philanthropy, are seen as the traditional way of supporting charity, sitting next to that are the companies who allow their staff to take a day's leave to volunteer with their charity of choice. This can be effective but unless it is engineered appropriately, it is a waste of time for the charity partner you are hoping to support. There are two ways in which this can play out positively. A staff member is already actively engaged with a charity in their own time and the company allows them a day off a year to continue that support. Is it making a big difference to that employee? I'd suggest not, as they were going to spend the time with the charity anyway—their track record has shown that. Now they just get to do it one day a year on company time.

The other way it can work well is when the resources are pulled together and there is a slight twist to the day. The Jellis Craig Group, a leading real estate network in Victoria, does this particularly well by visiting the Red Cross to donate blood as a company. Clearly it doesn't take a full day to do this, but what it does is allow the staff who participate a way of making a valuable contribution of their time.

The volunteer day goes a little astray, in my view, when the company gives someone time off to volunteer with a charity for a single day rather than as part of an ongoing commitment. Consider the productivity of someone stepping into your business for just one day. You take them through the induction, show them a video of what you do and what you stand for and then...what? The real risk is they become a burden to the charity, their personal experience is not an engaging or rewarding one, and the experience is quite negative for all involved. Once again there needs to be proper planning and purpose, otherwise you may as well give the staff a 'beach day' and call it what it is—just another day out of the office.

What about when you bring the resources together? When you have an organisation that has a workforce of more than 250 people you can start to leverage your volunteer days in a more effective way. Rather than every staff member taking their one annual day off, how about if those days were pooled and through a reward and recognition program a number of the team could take off one day per week to work with a charity partner who is part of the company's CSR program? If you had 50 staff donate their one day off and one of their team was able to combine those days, then you start to talk leverage. Now you have the same team member turning up to the same charity partner once a week for a year. Now there is real value for the charity partner and a meaningful opportunity for the volunteer. With a workforce of 250 plus, you can effectively do this across four charity partners, and now we are talking real change. What is the cost to the business? Well, it's the same as giving everyone in the business one day off—you are simply combining those days.

The other variation on volunteer days is to bring the team together for a combined purpose. Again this needs structure and respect. You may be a great accountant, salesperson or lawyer, but those skills won't qualify you to build houses for people in need. Would you be happy to have your home built by hairdressers or accountants? These types of programs need to delineate clearly between ability and ambition. But get them right and they can be the most amazing experiences you can have as a group.

Case study: Slums of Bangkok

One of the amazing life experiences I get to share as a keynote speaker and CSR consultant is seeing programs come to life and witnessing the difference it makes to those who really engage in a meaningful way.

Christopher J. Hegarty writes: 'To create a legacy is to plant a tree under which you will never sit. It is to look past your interests, your hopes and your lifetime . . . to put into motion changes that will be an indelible inspiration to those who follow'. Engaging in an authentic way, when the giving is the driving force, can and does create once-in-a-lifetime experiences.

In early 2013 I took a team of insurers from AIA Australia into the slums of Khlong Toei in Bangkok, where they spent the day creating their own legacy.

We started the morning with a keynote in which I set the context, talking about leadership, clarity of purpose and results without excuses. I didn't mention the word *perspective*, but I know that is a takeout from the sessions. Each of the delegates stepped out of their suit and corporate attire, put on their Hands t-shirt and boarded the waiting bus. They had no idea what was to come.

They weren't embarking on an organised tour. Nothing of the sort exists where we were heading. Travelling through the busy, crowded streets they quickly left behind the familiar sleek skyscrapers of the financial district and burrowed into the slums of Khlong Toei, the heartbeat of the real Bangkok.

Fiercely competitive in the business world, these 103 highly successful business operators and their life partners were undertaking a unique experience that would leave little footprints on their heart. At our destination each was greeted by the local kids, who draped a garland of flowers around their neck.

Their mission for the day was to transform a rundown kindergarten into the pride of the neighbourhood. They worked, they sweated and they toiled in the heat. Many couldn't remember the last time they had worked so hard physically. They not only embraced the challenge, but their engagement was on a level that was a privilege to be a part of. What was absent as these business heavyweights worked shoulder to shoulder in the most foreign of environments was any sign of competitiveness among them. There was something else too, something more intrinsic to our modern life. It dawned on me only late in the day that none of these leaders of business were checking their phones! Big deal? I think not. You watch any group of people today and the minute the conversation flags (you're lucky if they wait until then) they are on their phones. None of these guys checked their phones ever—all day. This was the level of engagement each of them felt with the project.

To see them down on their knees wiping the floor with rags after a day's work, to be down there with the National Manager, the two of us crawling around wiping up paint spots, was an amazing experience. And it brought so much to so many, even the kids in the new kindergarten benefiting.

What made the experience such a success:

- The project was worthwhile because the community benefited directly from it.

- The outcomes from the input of labour were visible and incontrovertible.

- The project offered meaningful opportunities for personal engagement.

- The work was within the skill capacity of those who participated.
- The experience was shared by all involved.

Employee engagement can take many forms. Too much time is spent on creating policy and procedure, and too much time is spent thinking and talking. The real value comes when you engineer opportunities for shared experiences. In this case the gift of giving was quite small, but the return to the 103 delegates who became dream makers that day was immeasurable.

Recently I ran into the National Manager at a conference in Shanghai where I was speaking, and she told me that day in Bangkok is still spoken about throughout the company as one of the most engaging experiences they have shared on conference.

Further strategies

There are many other ways that the corporate and for-purpose sectors can come together to bring about change. Business can provide goods and services to their charity partners at no cost or at heavily discounted rates. Offering pro-bono services to a charity is a great way to leverage the skills within a business and to meet their partners' needs. And this type of support is not confined to the large firms. Across Australia there are firms such as Sashi Veale & Associates, a small accountancy firm that has been contributing to the success of Hands for the past nine years through the provision of pro-bono accounting services.

The best way Sashi, the principal of the firm, can contribute is by leveraging the skills she and her team have as accountants. Is it the most rewarding experience for her and the team, just to do more of what they do every day, but without payment? Probably not, but they wanted to support the charity in the best way they could, not necessarily take away the best experience for themselves. This is another example of the value in being clear about what you are seeking from your involvement. If

Sashi and the team were looking for personal experiences from their involvement, they would be disappointed.

In looking to engage with their charity partner the business will build their strategy according to the many options that exist, some of which have been covered, but is there another way?

Absolutely there is. Optus, Australia's second largest telco, is an example of a company that, rather than going to a charity and asking where they need help or indeed inviting the charities to submit an application for assistance, identifies the problem they would like to put resources into and then goes looking for partners to help execute the strategy it has identified. It's a much more top-down approach and shows immense clarity in its commitment and what it is looking to take out of the relationship.

As Optus has shown, it's not always about giving or about working with other partners. Many of the changes that fall within the ambit of CSR can be made in isolation from the charity sector.

A company can include as part of their strategy a hiring policy that sees them take on a percentage of their employees from marginalised or disadvantaged groups. They may include a reduction in the use of their consumable resources such as power and water, or commit to reducing the landfill that leaves their manufacturing plants. These are all ways of committing to the wellbeing of the communities in which we live and work, and they will also return benefits to the business through reduced operating costs. Alternatively, as part of their strategy a company may choose to source raw materials from suppliers who meet certain employment standards, who return profits to the local community or who meet other conditions that see benefits flow back to communities.

The key points to consider when entering the sector include the following:

- Define the *why* of your reasons for wanting to enter the sector. When the business invests time in understanding why it wants to be involved and what it hopes to gain from the engagement, the path to realising its model becomes easier.

- Define the *strategy* for the engagement that will allow the team to execute it. There are many different opportunities and methodologies for engagement, and the greater the investment in building the engagement strategy, the greater the returns are likely to be.

- Consider the *give*—the different ways you can contribute, whether through cash donations, workplace giving or fundraising events. The most successful strategies are those that have a core focus on experiences but also the latitude and flexibility to cater for the diversity of the workforce.

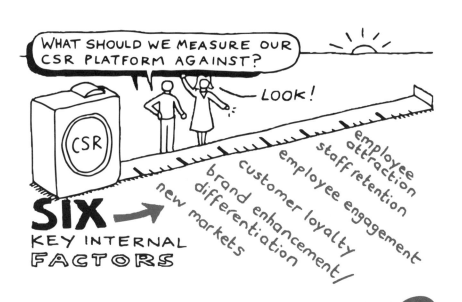

chapter 3

BUSINESS BENEFITS
of engagement

Not too many businesses are established for the sole purpose of supporting charities. There are exceptions, and smart charities are recognising the possible benefits here. Rather than relying on someone standing in the street shaking a can for donations, charities are creating 'for-profit' enterprises to support their charitable work.

I entered the charity sector in 2005 by forming the charity Hands Across the Water as a direct result of my exposure to a need that existed in Thailand following the Boxing Day tsunami. To say I was naive as to what was involved in establishing and running a charity would be to exaggerate my knowledge. But, in a story not uncommon to the evolution of small charities, I identified a need and decided I was well placed to address that need. Five years later I had learned enough to know that relying on donations was a limiting model and that there was an opportunity to do a couple of things differently. The first was that we would build our growth around the concept of creating shared experiences and the second was that we would invest in sustainability.

To ensure the growth of Hands continued, without compromising the position we had adopted of 100 per cent of donations going directly to the children and the projects in Thailand, we formed a company that sat next to the charity. The sole purpose of this company was to undertake commercial activities that would raise income to be used to meet the administration costs of the charity and allow for the employment of staff. Any excess funds would be donated to the charity entity. The company was not formed as a means of directing money to myself or the other directors; its constitution prohibits that. The reason it was formed was to remove the charity's total reliance on raising money by donations. It is a for-profit company formed purely to support charity.

> ...there was an opportunity to do a couple of things differently. The first was that we would build our growth around the concept of creating shared experiences and the second was that we would invest in sustainability.

Measurable returns: expect them and demand them

The formation of the company to support Hands might be a useful model for charities looking to spread their risk, but it is very much the exception when it comes to why companies are formed.

In the main, businesses are created and survive on their ability to meet the demand for goods they have to offer. Basic economics holds that if there is demand and you have supply you are in business. But it is never just about meeting an existing need; there has to be a consideration offered in return for the services. Early in our development that might have been food in exchange for labour, but for the most part we have advanced beyond that to work in a global currency, and built into that is a profit margin. This allows for a return on investment, business growth and reward for risk.

So when organisations, large and small, start looking to give to charity, shouldn't that exchange conform to the business model by offering a positive return on their investment?

You can hear them saying now, 'But we don't do it for a return, we do it to give back, we're good corporate citizens...', blah blah blah. You're not good corporate citizens, though. You're giving away profits that shareholders are entitled to, and if your giving is not attached to measurable returns, you're more likely than not an immature investor in this social sector space.

There are a number of problems associated with giving without expecting a positive return on the investment.

- Your giving without return will be known through the business as 'our community investment program' or something similar. Speak to the CFO and they will report it as a cost centre, a loss to the business. Sure, they will claim the tax deduction but it remains a cost to the business.

- You'll give while the going is good, but when times are hard and it comes time to reduce costs, guess what's first to be cut—the 'community investment program'.

Business benefits of engagement

- There is no building of a relationship between the charity partner and your company, which is giving the money away. Sure, there might be a nice morning tea when the cheque is handed over, or a grand evening with everyone dressed in their finest when the announcement is made in front of clients, colleagues and charity workers, and the CEO looks like a champion for the evening as he presents the big cheque.

- Within the business the relationship with the charity partner or the annual event is not going to receive dedicated resources or the interest of senior personnel. The work will be given to those in the comms area, or marketing or the EA can manage it, a bit like the staff Christmas party. No one gets too involved in the management of it, because at the end of the day 'it's not really what we're here to do, is it?'.

ALIGNMENT IS...

BUSINESS VALUES

CSR STRATEGY

... THE KEY TO SUCCESS!

It's in the interests of all parties to ensure there is an experience, there is engagement and the relationship continues beyond the donation.

I discuss in this chapter how those returns to the business can come about when we look at staff engagement surveys, retention rates, new markets, customer loyalty and so on, but here the analysis focuses on why it is not only appropriate but essential to expect the return.

Again, simply giving money to charity is one of the least valued forms of giving. From the charity's perspective, if I ask you for a donation and you give me a donation, regardless of size, that is often the end of the relationship. Sure, that donation greases the charity's wheels, allowing business to continue for a short time, but where do you go from there? It's in the interests of all parties to ensure there is an experience, there is engagement and the relationship continues beyond the donation.

One of the most powerful means of generating a return from the investment is to improve the engagement levels within the business. Plenty of research points to the multiplier effect on business when you have an engaged workforce as opposed to a disengaged one. Get them highly engaged and get yourself ready for serious growth.

If an engaged workforce is your ticket to increased morale and retention rates and higher standing as a desired employer, then one of the fastest ways to reach that place is through strategic investment in the charity sector. How do you measure that? How do you make it tangible? You ask the question the answer to which needs to satisfy the 'but for' test. Can you identify something that your investment has achieved that, 'but for' your investment, wouldn't have occurred? Basically, can you measure the difference you have made, not to your business, but to the charity? Can you report back that as a result of your involvement:

- 10 000 meals were provided to the homeless

- a radiograph was purchased and 500 x-rays performed, which diagnosed seven cases of cancer that would otherwise have gone undetected

- 2500 children in remote Australia were provided with school textbooks

- the Royal Flying Doctor service flew 700 hours and treated 94 patients

- a home, hospital or school was built as a direct result of your funding.

When this type of tangible outcome is provided internally and externally, there is much greater traction as people start to feel they are making a difference—and indeed the company they are working for is making a difference.

Charities have effectively dumbed this down for the consumer for years by claiming $3 a day will provide clean drinking water for a village or $100 will buy a goat. It's questionable whether it remains as effective today, but the strategy can certainly be flipped to demonstrate the difference being made and satisfy the 'but for' test.

> …there is much greater traction as people start to feel they are making a difference — and indeed the company they are working for is making a difference.

Jessica B. Rodell, a professor at the University of Georgia, has found in her research that 'when jobs are less meaningful, employees are more likely to increase volunteering to gain that desired sense of meaning'.

Effective CSR strategies are less about corporate philanthropy and increasingly about a strategic investment. Business exists for the fundamental reason of making a profit. Strip any business down to its purest reason for existence and if it isn't making a profit then its life is limited. The stronger the

Doing Good by Doing Good

business is, the better able it is to support those who rely on it. Without a strong business the ability to employ people, provide the goods and services it offers, return dividends to its shareholders and support the community is limited. The thought leaders in business are creating ways to ensure their CSR strategies are contributing to the growth and profitability of their companies.

Making a profit is seldom the sole reason for going into business, but it is from this core purpose that the other cascading effects of business flow. To this end, any CSR strategy that is not making the business money will be a cost centre and the first to go when business becomes tight owing to a shrinking economy, lack of consumer confidence or other negative influences on the demand for the goods and services offered.

> Making a profit is seldom the sole reason for going into business, but it is from this core purpose that the other cascading effects of business flow.

If part of the driving force behind setting up a CSR strategy is to bring support to the community, shouldn't we be ensuring that the community can rely on this support? In difficult economic times the demand on community groups servicing the social sector will increase as businesses close and people lose their jobs and/or find their disposable income shrinking. It is then that the demand for support from those providing the services will increase and that those providers will be looking to business and the corporate sector to step up their giving rather than roll it back.

If the CSR strategy is not making the company money, if it is seen simply as a 'nice to have' but a cost to the business, they will roll it back in the first round of cutbacks. This is why we need to ensure CSR is making the business money and that this can be readily identified. It also keeps the shareholders happy, which has to be a good thing.

Those entering the CSR space for the first time will often feel guilty, or at the very least feel it is the 'right thing' to reject the benefits of giving. I have found this particularly so when it comes to the giving of financial support. My response to this is, stop rejecting what is rightfully yours. Until the mindset that CSR is about 'giving back' shifts to one that sees it as an integrated part of the strategy of the business, everyone involved in the relationship chain is missing out. Without leveraging the full opportunities, the results never reach their potential.

> Until the mindset that CSR is about 'giving back' shifts to one that sees it as an integrated part of the strategy of the business, everyone involved in the relationship chain is missing out.

So how can giving be good for business? We can measure the return to business in both hard and soft returns.

The hard returns are those the accountants love to see and the CFO will take pleasure in reporting on. They are the dollars in the bank that can be attributed to the CSR strategy. The soft returns are less easy to quantify. If your program is supporting the 'clown doctors' at children's hospitals we can measure the number of visits they make to the sick kids; we can even break it down into the hours and children visited per sponsored shift, but how do we quantify the return of happiness in a terminally ill child? What's the value of the smile for a child who may not live out the year?

A simple model of business benefits

Let's consider the known returns and those that a successful CSR strategy should be bringing to your business. If you are new to the CSR space and are considering 'what's in it for me' or you are looking to see if the return is worth the investment, I suggest there are six key internal factors that should be measured against when considering the value of your CSR platform:

- employee attraction
- staff retention
- employee engagement
- customer loyalty
- brand enhancement/differentiation
- new markets.

The first three relate directly to your workforce and how it influences your ability to attract, retain and engage your employees. The next three relate to your position in the marketplace, influence on customer loyalty and new markets.

Figure 3.1 illustrates the basic model of how I see the benefits flow after years of working within this space and consulting to organisations building their programs. It very simply identifies where the benefits to business lie in six key areas.

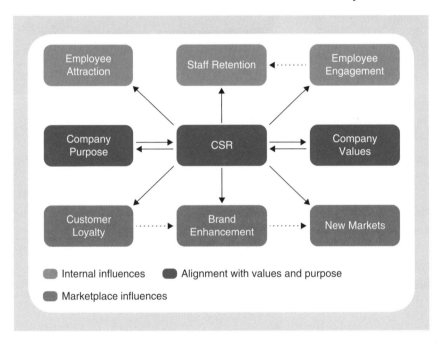

Figure 3.1: the flow-on benefits to business of engaging in the NFP sector

At the core of the model, and indeed the key to the success of any program, is alignment between the values and purpose of the business and its CSR strategy. In chapter 12 we consider the importance of alignment between the values and purpose and how they will guide investment in the CSR space. CSR is not an opportunity to 'buy credibility', which will quickly become obvious

> ... the key to the success of any program, is alignment between the values and purpose of the business and their CSR strategy.

both internally and in the marketplace, and will lead to greater cynicism and lack of trust. For there to be authenticity there needs to be alignment between a CSR program and business values.

This model demonstrates how the benefits will flow internally and externally into the market. It also shows the relationship that exists between the various groups. There is no question that an effective CSR platform will contribute to staff retention, and we look at that in much greater detail later. But we can also see how it will lead to enhanced staff engagement, which in turn leads to staff retention.

Let's now consider the six areas of positive benefit to a company when the CSR program is aligned, authentic and properly executed.

Employee attraction

It is no longer only the consumer who is concerned with more than just a business's profit-making; job seekers, particularly those new to the workforce, are more than mildly interested in the social behaviour of the company they are looking to work with. And many of those entering the workforce for the first time come with a fair degree of cynicism built into their DNA. In generations gone by the prospective employee might have looked first at securing the job, and felt fortunate to have done so, and only then asked 'what can I expect to be paid and will I get four weeks' annual leave?'

Now they are asking, 'If I take your job, how long before I get promoted and what are you doing to improve the lives of those outside this company? Tell me the difference you are making to the things that are important to me'.

As important as it is to have a strategy to engage and retain staff, we accept they will leave, and the evidence is that this will happen more often over the next five years as the economy continues to improve and the global labour market becomes more fluid. In building engagement programs to retain staff, the value is also in your ability to attract the talent you desire in an increasingly competitive space. Paying higher salaries is not the answer. The point of leverage quickly becomes unsustainable if that is the only tool in the toolbox you have to draw on, and we know that's not what motivates people. There needs to be a differentiator: an authentic CSR strategy can give you an edge over your competitors.

Research conducted by the Cone Millennial Cause group, detailed in *The 2020 Workplace* report, found that 80 per cent of a sample of 1800 13- to 25-year-olds wanted to work for a company that cares about how it impacts on and contributes to society. More than half said they would refuse to work for an irresponsible corporation.

Not only does the investment a company makes in CSR make it more attractive to prospective talent, but once they are on board it enables staff development through opportunities that otherwise might not present.

Staff retention

The performance of the global economy is a major factor in staff retention. Between 2010 and 2012 staff retention rates remained consistent; however, predictions are that as the economy again begins to heat up, many employees who have been biding their time will get ready to head for the doors. If companies haven't been focusing on staff retention in the past, they certainly need to do so now to avoid losing valuable talent and incurring the significant costs of replacing them and the loss of productivity that goes with each employee as they walk out the door.

Research conducted by Hay Group suggests that the spike in turnover will be sharpest in the developing countries of Asia and Latin America, while more mature markets are likely to feel that spike between 2014 and 2018. Analysis by Hay Group suggests that Australia can expect a turnover rate of around 22 per cent, with the USA slightly higher and Canada slightly lower at 20 per cent. They predict that many developing Asian countries can expect a turnover rate of between 25 and 30 per cent, with the impact expected to be felt sooner than in the developed countries.

To mitigate these losses, remember that there are a number of things that drive staff to remain in their current workplace, including:

- leadership of the organisation
- alignment of values between employee and company
- fair reward
- growth potential
- the right people in the right roles.

Jeff Swartz, CEO of Timberland, has suggested that employees 'don't stay with a company because of benefits. It is the long-term relationship-building that attracts people to stay'. Just because Timberland was a leader in this area, he added, it didn't mean their employee retention was 'marginally better' than other companies' because of this commitment. Instead, he said, it was the company's culture to promote innovation, engagement and employee input that factored much higher in an employee's decision to leave or stay.

As Richard Welford discusses in *CSR Asia Weekly*, many businesses do not give enough consideration to the costs associated with staff turnover. Staff retention is also a huge problem. He says that costs include those associated with recruitment, such as advertising for a new position, and lost productivity when an employee leaves their position, can hurt a business.

Exit surveys of some 11 000 employees from 40 Australian companies over a four-year period by Australian-based research group Insync Surveys found that there has been very little environmental change in the reasons for people leaving their employment and, interestingly, that organisations and their leaders have a massive opportunity to reduce that turnover. They estimate that the cost of turnover per employee amounts to 75 per cent of their annual salary when all factors are considered. Whatever numbers you work with, and whoever your favourite industry researcher is, the fact is inescapable that huge savings can be made by hanging on to your valued employees.

CSR is not the solution to staff turnover. It alone won't stop people leaving your organisation, but if it can deepen the level of engagement and in turn prevent even a small percentage of your team from looking elsewhere, the investment will be worthwhile on that basis alone.

Employee engagement

The statistics around the proportion of the workforce that is engaged, disengaged and actively disengaged vary between researchers and across countries and industries. Levels of engagement reported vary from as low as 30 per cent to as high as 60 per cent, with the remainder of the workforce either disengaged or actively disengaged. The actively disengaged employee not only will be unhappy in their workplace but will express their disapproval of the company or their employer through their actions and language. The potential of their behaviour to disrupt and infect others, like a virus making its way through the air conditioning, cannot be measured.

While the research conclusions differ, what is consistent is the negative impact of disengagement and the benefits of an effective CSR strategy in building employee engagement.

'Research shows that engaged employees are more productive employees,' Gallup Strategic Consulting reports. 'They are more profitable, more customer-focused, safer, and more likely to withstand temptations to leave the organization. In the best organizations, employee engagement transcends a human resources initiative—it is the way they do business. Employee engagement is a strategic approach supported by tactics for driving improvement and organizational change. The best performing companies know that developing an employee engagement strategy and linking it to the achievement of corporate goals will help them win in the marketplace.'

The engagement of employees will be enhanced by their belief in the commitment of the company to more than making a profit. When an organisation demonstrates a real awareness and interest in their needs beyond the balance sheet, employees' commitment to that company grows. It's about believing that the company cares. And if it cares about the needs of society, then there's a good chance it cares about its staff as well.

As reported by *CA Magazine* (May 2010), a study into CSR by the global human resources consulting and outsourcing firm Hewitt Associates drew some interesting conclusions.

The study revealed that it is important to be consistent and sustain a CSR strategy over the long term, in combination with other employee engagement boosters such as competitive compensation, and good management and health and safety practices. The perception of a decline in CSR performance was said to be a significant threat to engagement for a third of the employees surveyed. Combined initiatives to both sustain employee engagement and support CSR transformation will most likely yield a better return on investment than individual non-coordinated efforts.

There is a strong link between employee engagement and the way employees view their employers' corporate social responsibility approach. 'Anecdotally we know younger or "Gen Y" employees are very interested in working for companies that are "green". What we confirmed through the study is that employees of all ages want their employer to behave ethically, support their communities and work to reduce their environmental impacts,' says Barb Steele, director of membership, Canadian Business for Social Responsibility (CBSR).

> There is a strong link between employee engagement and the way employees view their employers' corporate social responsibility approach.

Hewitt Associates found that 35 per cent of those surveyed would take a 15 per cent pay cut to work for a company committed to CSR, 45 per cent agreed to the same pay cut if their job made a positive social or environmental impact while 58 per cent would sacrifice 15 per cent of their income to work for an organisation with values that matched theirs.

Customer loyalty

The question of whether a company's CSR position does more than positively influence consumers' attitudes is an important one. We need to know if it results in a change in consumer *behaviour*. Are they willing to pay more or change brand based on a company's CSR position? One sector that trades heavily on its environmental morality is the game and livestock industry. Do consumers really understand what is meant by 'free range' and 'organic', and does the labelling influence consumer behaviour?

Researchers Kusum L. Ailawadi and Jackie Luan from the Tuck School of Business at Dartmouth, New Hampshire, set out to quantify how much CSR benefits a company, using the consumer goods retail sector as a testing ground and 3000 grocery shoppers as subjects. The study measured consumers' perceptions of retailers across four CSR performance dimensions (environmental friendliness, treating employees fairly, community support and sourcing from local growers/ suppliers) and several attributes (such as price, quality and assortment). Here's what the researchers discovered:

- All four CSR performance dimensions positively influence consumer attitudes.

- Consumers modify purchase behaviour only when the CSR benefit directly affects their experience with the company or brand (broad categories such as 'environmentally friendly' build goodwill but specific, relatable initiatives such as 'locally sourced' increase spending).

- Improving consumer perception on a CSR dimension just a little (one point on a five-point scale) can result in a lift in sales of 10 to 15 per cent on average.

- There are opportunities to add a price premium (between 12 and 16 per cent) for brands/products with CSR benefits.

- Consumers prefer CSR-oriented retailers because they see personal benefit from the CSR initiatives and the initiatives resonate with their values.

Brand enhancement/differentiation

The modern charity needs to shift its focus on fundraising from one of asking for money and making the donor feel guilty to one of involving the donor in the value exchange. It needs to offer either an experience that donors and supporters can be a part of or a product that drives their income. A strategy that is increasing in popularity is partnership, or at the very least the licensed use of the charity name and logo by companies who want to enhance their brand or differentiate themselves in the marketplace while at the same time driving sales.

There are several layers to the benefits to brand and image that companies can derive from their involvement in the social sector. But for it to work it needs to be a strategic investment aligned to the values of the organisation with close proximity to its core business. A high degree of effort and integrity and more than a touch of modesty are required to achieve a positive outcome.

In her research paper 'Strategic CSR acts as insurance for reputation, which improves financial performance', Lauren Rakowski, from the Network for Business Sustainability, found that consumers' 'purchase intentions were twice as high for products of companies described as having a strong CSR reputation compared with those with a weak CSR reputation following a product recall'. The benefit of CSR even without a product recall was derived from investing in the 'insurance' of the goodwill afforded the company by their commitment to CSR.

Rakowski further drew three main implications for those choosing to drive CSR through their organisation. Firstly, there was a need to develop long-term relationships with social causes by engaging their employees with volunteer programs, providing access to resources and donating to those causes. Building those longer term relationships demonstrated a commitment by the company, and it is this long-term commitment that helps build reputation.

The second implication was that the company act with modesty in their involvement in the social space. Rakowski found that many leading brands, such as Citibank and GE, valued discreet support for social causes. She found that tobacco company Phillip Morris was criticised for spending more money promoting its charitable donations than actually donating.

The third consideration was that the company align its giving and support to the industry in which it is operating or be selective in the number of causes it chooses to align itself with. Rakowski found in her research that stakeholders see actions as 'less self-serving' when donations are made to fewer and less generic causes.

This final point shouldn't be a surprise, as it becomes easier for both sides to identify the impact made when it can be measured through a well-structured campaign. For the company giving their resources, whether staff time or financial, it is easier to track the changes that are brought about by dividing 100 000 units of their donation between two or three charity partners than it is by dividing those 100 000 units across 50 partners. The success of a CSR strategy is measured not in the units of giving alone but in the change that has occurred on both sides of the ledger.

There is a flip side to the benefits of promoting your company as a good corporate citizen that cares for its people and the communities in which they live. Jay Janney and Steve Gove in their 2011 paper 'Reputation and Corporate Social Responsibility Aberrations, Trends and Hypocrisy', for the *Journal of Management Studies*, reached a number of conclusions. The first, that organisations who have a strong reputation for CSR will be partially buffered from scandal, we already know. The inverse of this, however, is that 'when firms possess an enhanced reputation for CSR associated with corporate governance, violations pertaining specifically to governance are viewed as hypocritical and more harshly sanctioned'.

> The success of a CSR strategy is measured not in the units of giving alone but in the change that has occurred on both sides of the ledger.

Building your brand around the social sector is as close as it gets to running a business to support a charity. In the case of TOMS, for example, was the company created to address the social need, with profit being secondary, or was it the reverse, with the motivator being to build a successful for-profit company by tapping into the desire of consumers to do more socially? Either way, the company is an example of tapping into the desires of consumers to do more when they spend and of how that can drive phenomenal growth.

TOMS founder Blake Mycoskie gives himself the title 'Chief Shoe Giver'. The TOMS website is confusing: is it a cutting-edge charity that has hit a niche market of selling shoes to support its endeavours or it is a commercial entity that is changing the way of giving? And that confusion is the greatest compliment that can be given to an organisation. The secret, of course, is the greater the company's commercial success the greater their giving power, and at TOMS it could not be framed in simpler terms: you buy one pair of shoes or sunglasses from them and they will give one pair of shoes or sunglasses on your behalf to someone in need. Simply brilliant.

New markets

Bill Gates talks about 'creative capitalism — an approach where governments, NFPs, and business work together to stretch the reach of market forces so that more people can make a profit, or gain recognition, doing work that eases the world's inequities'.

There are many success stories of companies entering new markets on the back of CSR, particularly in the developing world. Several leading examples of these are offered by pharmaceutical companies who, by providing aid and supporting development for those on the ground, have opened up new markets for them. The question of whether the new market they were able to enter was always their strategic reason for the investment or rather was an unforeseen outcome I think is simply answered. The new markets they enter are not opened by accident. The clear message, though, is that CSR can and should deliver positive returns to an organisation, and those who invest heavily will derive the rewards.

Researchers Mark Little and Adam Lane from Business for Social Responsibility wrote about this for *BSR Insight*, in an article titled 'Using CSR to Enter New Markets'. They discussed how the world's largest company focused on diabetes, Novo Norodisk, entered the diabetes market in China and decided to leverage a long-term CSR strategy alongside its products. Its strategy focused on health, economic development and the environment, and included building of diabetes clinics and prevention programs around the country. One of its economic aims is to use local manufacturers to support the Chinese market in the near future.

Pfizer uses its support of capacity building within the NGO sector by placing 200 of its staff on a six-month deployment in 36 countries around the world. The Pfizer staff work with the leaders of the NGOs and in doing so gain invaluable local intelligence in those markets that would not otherwise be available to them. This intelligence then allows the company to build strategies for penetrating these new markets.

This chapter looks at the benefits to business of engaging with the NFP sector and what types of returns they can and should expect. These include:

- **Employee attraction.** Job seekers, particularly those new to the workforce, are more than mildly interested in the social behaviour of the company they are looking to work with. There needs to be a differentiator, and an authentic CSR strategy can give you the edge over your competitors.

- **Staff retention.** A CSR program alone won't stop staff from leaving. But a meaningful, well-engineered CSR strategy that engages staff will contribute to staff retention.

- **Employee engagement.** When an organisation demonstrates a real awareness and interest in needs beyond the balance sheet, the employee's commitment to that company grows. It's about believing that the company cares. And if it cares about the needs of society, then there's a good chance it cares about its staff as well.

- **Customer loyalty.** Research shows that consumers prefer CSR-oriented retailers, and that an improved customer perception of a company based on its CSR can result in sales increases and opportunities to add a price premium.

- **Brand enhancement/differentiation.** There are several layers to the benefits to brand and image that companies can derive from their involvement in the social sector. But for it to work it needs to be a strategic investment aligned to the values of the organisation and with close proximity to the core business of the organisation. Achieving a positive outcome also requires a high degree of effort and integrity and more than a touch of modesty.

- **New markets.** By addressing the needs in previously untapped markets that may have been considered no-go areas because of commercial difficulties, companies that are brave enough to accept the challenge find new distribution channels, and often these are driven by innovation.

chapter 4

SMALL BUSINESS:
the multiplier effect

You don't have to be big to make a difference. You don't have to have a massive organisation behind you to have an effective CSR program. There is no invisible threshold that needs to be reached before you start contributing to your favourite charity or the broader community.

The story of TOMS shoes, featured in chapter 6, illustrates how a venture can start from nothing on the basis of addressing a need that existed from day one. If you wait until you have reached a certain profit margin or annual turnover goal before you start contributing, all you are doing is delaying your entry and missing opportunities. The thought that 'we will once we have' is based on the limited view that getting involved is a one-way process. The sooner you get involved, the sooner that old paradigm can be overturned by a new way of doing things, one that will stretch your mind. For many, *doing good by doing good* is a reality they need to experience to believe in. It's certain, though, that if you do nothing, then nothing will change.

> For many, *doing good by doing good* is a reality they need to experience to believe in.

WordStorm: the value of in-kind support

WordStorm is a Sydney-based PR agency specialising in media relations and social media for entrepreneurial-driven organisations. Its team of six is smaller than the staff some of the larger corporates profiled in this book have working full-time on their CSR strategies alone! But that doesn't mean they can't make a difference and it doesn't mean that this difference isn't hugely significant.

Monica Rosenfeld founded WordStorm in 2000 with a very clear strategy of supporting charity. 'We really wanted to engage with an organisation on a deeper level than just handing over cash, besides the fact that as a small business we don't have a lot of extra cash to donate to a specific cause. We see donating our time and using our expertise in the area of PR as something that will bring about real benefits.' Monica's position here is typical of many small businesses. Despite their desire to do so, they just don't have the tolerance of larger businesses who can contribute vast sums of money to charity. It's this lack of capacity, though, that sees them engaging in a more meaningful way and bringing about greater change than would otherwise be likely, even if they contributed the same value in cash as their in-kind support is worth.

Hands Across the Water was fortunate to be picked up as a client by WordStorm. Monica recalls how that came about: 'Divine intervention and serendipity really! I read your book over the Christmas holidays in 2011–12 and then happened to bump into an old school friend who had just visited one of the orphanages you had built in Thailand over the same Christmas holidays. She invited me to come to the gala dinner with her and I took my husband and business partner, Joram. During the dinner we both had a strong feeling of wanting to contribute WordStorm's services to Hands as we felt that was where we could personally be most effective in helping the organisation'.

Even before the series of fortunate events that saw Monica find her way to Hands, she was clear that contributing to an organisation was going to involve something beyond the donation of money. She was convinced the best opportunity was for her to create an experience for her staff and to leverage their knowledge and expertise. Monica's approach with Hands was to treat the charity as any other client and offer the same level of skill, resources and expertise she did her paying clients. Weekly reports are sent to the charity detailing what has occurred with the various campaigns they are running and forecasting the work they will be doing in the coming week. The team sets aside several hours each quarter for an update and overview with the management team of Hands to ensure the campaigns are in line with our direction, review the success and explore upcoming opportunities.

Monica's approach to her CSR work has returned results to WordStorm very quickly, which reflects the mature view that was taken when deciding to engage with a charity partner. Asked what it had done for engagement levels within the team, Monica replies, 'They are totally delighted with the work we do for Hands, and in every performance review we've done since working with Hands they've mentioned that it's one of the campaigns that gives them the most job satisfaction'.

But what of the results for Hands from the relationship? Has this level of in-kind support been beneficial for us? In our last annual catch-up we went through the reams and reams of articles that WordStorm had secured for us in major publications. From the glossy mags and major weekend national papers through to radio and television, the exposure has been huge. What would that be worth in dollars if we had to pay for it? Somewhere in the vicinity of $120 000. But the real value we have derived from the relationship goes well beyond even the dollar value of the media real estate we have been able to secure.

From experience I know that some people need multiple touch points before they will respond. Often I will hear from someone who has heard a keynote presentation, read about Hands in a magazine article and been to a dinner or seen an interview on television. It is the fact that we *keep* coming up in their lives that causes them to respond. Monica's personal story absolutely reflects this experience. She read the book, came to our Night of Celebration gala dinner and then decided to reach out.

What the team at WordStorm has been able to do for Hands is create many touch points for people of different demographics. We have been featured in seniors magazines and have had plenty of coverage in teen magazines too, with everything in between. During our 800 km rides in Thailand I like to explore how each of our riders has found their way to us, because the charity sector is such a crowded market. In 2014 we had a rider whose story went like this: he read an article about us in a magazine, which prompted him to learn more, so he bought the book *Hands Across the Water* and read that, then he decided he would ride with us in January 2014; such was his experience in 2014 that he is returning in 2015 to ride with his wife. Hands stands to receive a minimum of $30 000 in financial return from just this one rider. We haven't even considered the flow-on effect of who he has been able to reach in telling his story during the fundraising. We know his first touch point was the article. The rest has grown from there.

Has the relationship with WordStorm benefited Hands? Without question. Is the in-kind support that we receive from WordStorm of greater value to Hands than the same amount in a cash donation? Again, without question. If Monica turned around tomorrow and offered us $50 000 in cash or another year of support from her team, we would have no hesitation in taking the support from her team. The leverage that is possible has a multiplier effect. We are better off for it, as is Monica and WordStorm.

Does Monica see the value derived from the relationship as a profit or cost centre to the business? 'Neither,' she replies. 'It's more a "feel-good centre", which I guess results in more profit if the team is thriving and motivated.' They are *doing good by doing good*.

The key lessons and recommendations that Monica shares from her involvement with Hands are as follows:

- It's important to work with the right organisation and for the right reasons for your business.

- It's a wonderful way to enhance your business and to make a difference at the same time.

- Involving the team in the project is very satisfying for them and increases their overall motivation for the work they do within the business.

- It's important to choose an organisation that you feel you align with from a cultural and KPI point of view.

Churchill Education: connecting through shared personal values

'When the time comes to cut spending, we write a list of what can never be compromised on and it looks like this: provide for the Churchill families, provide for our family, provide for our charity family. The rest is on the table and up for grabs, but those three, they are untouchable.' And the charity family for Churchill Education continues to grow.

Churchill Education began operations in January 2006. It was founded by retired police officer Randall Smith and his wife Tricia Velthuizen, a former barrister of the Supreme Court of Queensland. Through a series of events this husband-and-wife team decided to leave their careers of putting crooks behind bars and start up a business that helps people receive the recognition their professional experience warrants.

Churchill Education operates in both the Australian and international markets helping their clients to obtain Australian qualifications through translating experience into qualifications, and through teaching further skills and knowledge relevant to industry. Their operations across Australia, the US and the Philippines currently employ 32 people.

They didn't start the business as a vehicle to support charity, but giving to those in need was always going to be a non-negotiable part of their existence. There are many reasons for having a CSR strategy in place and the depth of integration into businesses varies considerably. Josephine Sukkar, principal at Buildcorp, a long-time philanthropist and sought-after charity board member, believes that 'CSR will not work within business unless you have a champion and the owner of the business or someone at the top of the tree driving it'. Both Randall and Tricia at Churchill Education have a strong commitment to their chosen charities, which ensures that giving is part of the DNA of their business, and not surprisingly it is very successful.

> 'CSR will not work within business unless you have a champion and the owner of the business or someone at the top of the tree driving it.'

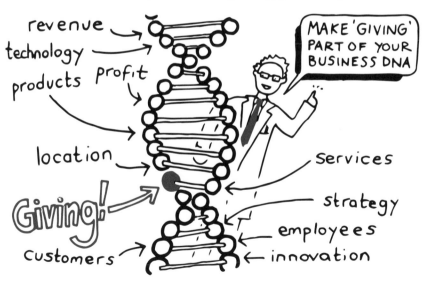

Giving to charity can be linked to the idea of 'I will when I have', which could be 'when net profit exceeds x' or 'when we have x millions in cash reserves' or 'when we have x staff as part of the team'. All of these limiting conditions are based on the premise that giving is a cost to the business. The giving at Churchill Education started as soon as the doors were opened, and anyone who has been part of a start-up business knows that at times, particularly early in the evolution of a business, cash flow can be tough.

When Tricia and Randall walked away from their careers they had 10 months' savings to cover their business and living expenses. Things were tight and they had got down to their last mortgage payment, ready to start looking for jobs again, when they landed a contract that set them up to continue the journey they are now on. But even through those first months, giving was part of their culture and part of the way they did business.

> 'We found that giving when it hurts was a powerful tool to ground us and to find gratitude for all that we have.'

As the business grew so did their level of giving. The portfolio of charities they support, and not in an insignificant way, has grown considerably for such a relatively small company. Their giving started with a connection formed by Tricia, and their overall strategy was driven by the two business owners. Their giving was ad hoc; there was no structure to the timing, which depended mainly on when they received a request. 'We progressively added other programs to our monthly commitments as we connected with a purpose, and continued to give on an ad hoc basis as need presented. We also actively sought out opportunities to give whenever business got a bit tough as a way of renewing our commitment from those very first days in business. We found that giving when it hurts was a powerful tool to ground us and to find gratitude for all that we have.'

Each of the staff who joined the growing team of Churchill Education was inducted in the giving, but few of them had a real say in the direction of the program, who should be supported and at what level. All of that changed in early 2014 when a decision was made to form a foundation that would shift the power from Tricia and Randall to the team that would have equal representation across the company and would set the direction for their giving.

Churchill Education Foundation supports charities in all sectors, the giving occurring at international, national and local levels. The rationale they adopted for their giving was that they have a business presence locally, nationally and internationally so their giving should be across all these areas too. 'In any business, where you find your community you also find your commitment,' Randall explains. 'As our world has become more connected, our reach has changed. It is no longer restricted to how far you can see to the horizon. The horizon has moved beyond our eyes, which has given us the opportunity to serve people we may never see but whose lives we can add value to.'

When it comes to selecting charity partners Randall and Tricia have previously made a decision based on a number of criteria. The first and foremost, though, is 'because they connect with us around our personal values'. Their commitment is to connecting the most vulnerable communities to education.

As they explain the process, 'it usually goes like this:

1   See a need.

2   Identify an organisation that can meet that need (often steps 1 and 2 happen simultaneously).

3   Decide to support that organisation in meeting that need.

4   Look at the accounts.

5   Decide it just means selling x more services to achieve this.

6   Share the commitment with the team.

7   Drive the sales to cover it'.

The most interesting are steps 1 and 2. Through various levels of exposure they come across the need, then they look for the right organisation to meet that need. This is very similar to the approach taken by Optus. As noted earlier, it too would identify a need and then look to work with the right partner to address the need. Churchill Education's strategic approach here represents the kind of thoughtful and mature thinking not often found in small to medium enterprises when selecting charity partners. The vast majority starting their CSR program will form an attachment to a charity rather than a cause. The approach of charity first, cause second is not necessarily wrong, but it can at times limit the breadth of choices that should be considered based on your governing principles.

I have met few people as personally committed to giving of themselves and all they have to those in need as Randall and Tricia. They have a process through which they make their charity decisions, but they look to find a way to make the cause fit within their very loose framework so they can say 'yes' more often than 'no'. And they give until it hurts, then give some more. As Tricia sees it, 'We are a river, not a dam. Opportunity and wealth come to us not to stall or stagnate, but to be a blessing to others downstream from us'.

They give because it is the right thing to do, but they are smart enough to know that it is also good for business. They optimise the concept of *doing good by doing good*. Asked to reflect on the return of their CSR program to their business their response, in summary, is this:

- It grounds us, reminding us of how fortunate we are and how much we have to give, which makes us more effective in making business decisions, giving us all the opportunity to reflect and to be kinder to each other and to our immediate community.

- It strengthens our team. They are not working just for us but for the betterment of their communities, which gives them something to be proud of.

- It drives us. When we revisit the budget, CSR is a non-negotiable aspect of it, so it forces us to do more business.

- It teaches us. We see how charities are making a difference in their communities, and that teaches us principles that we can use in our business.

- It opens doors. We have built relationships with some very inspiring people who through their leadership encourage us to be more, to be people our children can be proud of.

- It makes us more appealing when recruiting staff.

- It makes us more trustworthy in the eyes of our customers, although we have never shared the full extent of our giving with them.

'We are a river, not a dam. Opportunity and wealth come to us not to stall or stagnate, but to be a blessing to others downstream from us.'

What is most pleasing here is to see a small company, for whom giving has been a part of the way they do business since they first opened their doors, reap what they sow. They are enjoying the benefits of a more engaged team. Their staff retention is higher and they are more attractive to potential employees. As a result they are seeing increased customer loyalty and new business is coming their way.

Here are the three recommendations that Tricia and Randall would give to a business looking to implement a CSR program:

1 **Create connection.** Choose a charity that meets a need you feel a personal connection with. There are so many worthy charities, which can make choosing just one a little daunting. But when you find a charity you have a personal connection with, or that resonates with your company's mission and place in the business world, you are more likely to invest yourself and not just your money. To be effective over the long term, charities need more than just

money; they need believers to encourage them and hold them to account. Connect with them, and you will achieve so much more than just funding services.

2   **Create certainty.** Commit to giving with regularity. Like businesses, charities need a regular injection of cash to plan for the future and be more effective, to thrive and not merely survive. It creates certainty for you and the charity, makes you each significant in the other's world and builds a deeper connection between you.

3   **Create significance.** Give more than you feel entirely comfortable giving. This becomes a gift of faith, a gift from what is truly important to you, rather than just from your leftovers or hand-me-downs. And when you invest in someone from a place of value, it becomes a gift that you care about, a gift that you really want to see valued in return, creating a significant legacy. You will be more committed to sharing this significant investment with your team and your community. This in turn will generate even greater benefits for your charity partner and your community.

- You don't have to be a large organisation with a massive budget to get involved in the charity sector. If you delay your giving or entry into this space until you have reached a self-imposed financial position, you are just delaying the benefits that flow back to you.

- The returns to small business are very similar to the returns to big business. Staff engagement, new markets, customer loyalty and brand enhancement are not confined to big business. Small business can and does enjoy meaningful returns.

- Find a charity that aligns with the values of the business and the business owners. For small to medium enterprises the relationship with charity partners will be a lot more personal than for larger organisations. It is important to ensure an alignment of values not just with the business, but with the individuals.

- Involve the team in the giving process. Invite them to be part of making the decision on who will be supported and to contribute themselves, either in kind or financially.

chapter 5

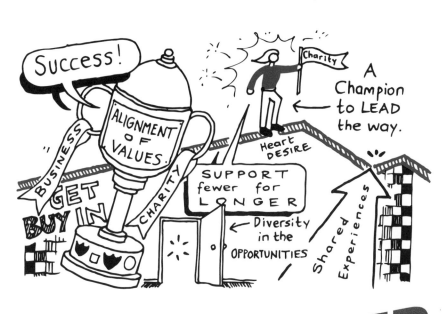

MEDIUM-SIZED BUSINESS:
aligning values and purpose

The myth that you need to be a large corporate before you can contribute or leverage the value of your CSR program was debunked in the previous chapter when I looked at WordStorm and Churchill Education. Both are small businesses, with six and 30 staff respectively, and both make contributions to the sector in their own way. WordStorm leverages its expertise within the business, running a full PR campaign for its chosen charity. Churchill Education has taken the approach of sharing its revenue with a number of different charities.

The two case studies in this chapter introduce Jellis Craig, a real estate company in Victoria that operates in the mid to top end of the market, and the National Associated Retail Traders of Australia (Narta), which has 32 members across Australia and is the largest independent electrical buying group in Australasia. The Narta model is quite different: as a buying group its members include many household names in retailing such as Myer, Bing Lee, JB Hi-Fi, David Jones, Retravision, Winning Appliances, Radio Rentals, Videopro, E & S Trading and many more. Its suppliers in the electrical retail space include Fujifilm, Beko, Miele, Samsung, Panasonic, LG, Fisher & Paykel, Electrolux and Smeg, among others. What makes the Narta model unique in part is that despite such a diverse group of members and suppliers, many of whom will have their own internal CSR programs and chosen charity partners, it has still been able to create a very meaningful program.

Jellis Craig: a multilayered approach

On the continuum that represents the journey from beginning to fully integrated shared value model (see chapter 9 for further discussion), the Jellis Craig Group is really just starting its journey. Its commitment to the charity sector is not new, but realising it wasn't reaching its potential it arrived at a point of reflection where it felt compelled to weigh up whether to end its support or to start again. Many beneficiaries will be pleased that it made the decision to recommit and reinvent its presence.

Jellis Craig is a real estate group with 12 offices spread across the inner suburbs of Melbourne, Victoria. It also has a presence on the coast and an office in the Macedon Ranges, providing coverage for their clients from 'Country to Coast'. The group was founded 23 years ago, first setting up in Hawthorn where it targeted the top end of the residential market based on premium properties and premium service. For 10 years it dominated that market. In more recent years it has expanded and restructured, which has allowed it to create greater scale.

It appeals to the mid to upper end of the residential sales market, which it supports with a large property management group. The restructure it underwent wasn't so much to grow the business in terms of its footprint across Melbourne, as to allow it to better serve the areas in which it operated. It doesn't seek to be the 'exclusive' brand, yet it is not aiming to grow to a group with 40 to 50 agencies either. It has found its place in the market and it is pretty happy with how it performs and how it services its clients. The approach to its business very much reflects the approach to its corporate social responsibility strategy. It's about making an investment in its people and the way they do business, focusing on making what they do successful rather than on growth for growth's sake.

The decision to invest in the CSR strategy was led by the CEO, Nick Dowling. Nick himself did not have a real estate background but joined the Jellis Craig Group (JCG) after a successful career in banking. After 18 months in the chair as CEO, Nick turned his attention to the relationship they had with their charity partner. It didn't feel to him that they were operating as effectively in this area as in their core business. He decided that if it couldn't be done properly they shouldn't be doing it all. Nick observed early on that no one on either side was benefiting as they might have done. 'The Jellis Craig Group had never lacked the heart or the desire; what was missing was someone to pull it all together.' He acknowledged it had nothing to do with the charity they were supporting; the relationship mirrored your typical corporate philanthropic

> It's about making an investment in their people and the way they do business, focusing on making what they do successful rather than growth for growth's sake.

approach. 'The charity we were supporting is a fantastic charity and doing great work. But we were giving money each year and really there wasn't much more to it from an engagement point of view.'

The path that JCG decided to travel was to set up its own foundation, which would allow it to take a structured approach to its charity partnerships. It was looking for something that offered opportunities for deeper engagement and that created shared experiences. From early on the plan was for a multilayered approach that would see them support two to three charities each year. The top tier of the approach would be to tackle a significant project that allowed them a level of involvement that went beyond merely giving money—a commitment that had a clear outcome.

From the beginning they recognised that by selecting one charity as the major beneficiary of your support you run the risk of alienating those who, for whatever reason, aren't on board with that project or who have their own cause with which they are passionately connected. Layering of support across a number of tiers created the opportunity for increased engagement with a greater number of the staff.

The major project, which was in partnership with Hands Across the Water to fund the construction of a home for children in need in Thailand, resonated strongly with the majority of the staff and offered many engagement options. The real difference to this project was they would be able to track the build process, see the kids move into the home and, over the period of their commitment, be very much involved in the lives of the children they were supporting.

> Layering of support across a number of tiers created the opportunity for increased engagement with a greater number of the staff.

Selecting Hands as the first major charity partner to benefit from their support under the new structure might not have made sense to some. Here is a Melbourne-based company whose main focus is on medium to high-end real estate choosing to support a Thailand-based charity. But the connection was in fact quite deep on a values level. The Jellis Craig Group is about putting people into homes, helping people realise their dreams. In Thailand, in conjunction with Hands, they are doing the same thing. They are putting kids into homes who otherwise would face a very desperate life, helping the children realise their dreams of having somewhere safe to live and food to eat a couple of times a day. At first glance it might not make sense, but when you look a little deeper, it couldn't be more aligned to what the Jellis Craig Group does every day in the suburbs of Melbourne.

One of the real advantages of the project was it gave them a tangible outcome of their support. 'We see the orphanage as a great opportunity. It connects with us on many levels around improving the lives of others. We are not the experts at doing this and we need to ensure we are not distracted from our core business. If we can work with a partner such as Hands, then we will be able to see it, feel it, touch it and even visit it by sending people over. We've already seen the benefit that two of our directors had from the Hands bike ride. Many of us just can't believe the difference the experience has meant to them and the change that has resulted.'

When he embarked on the journey of implementing a CSR platform Nick understood that it would take resources away from the core business and that for this reason it needed to be done effectively. 'As a commercial business it would be easier from a time perspective just to channel off a portion of the share of profits that we make every year, and feel good about it. But what I know from past experience is that you don't really feel good about the donation. And this is in no way a reflection on the charity partner; it's about the experiences that are created.'

When balancing the costs and benefits to the business of the reallocation of resources, Nick knew that if it was done appropriately the benefits that would be returned to the business would far outweigh the costs. He saw it as a key point of difference—one of the things that would separate the Jellis Craig Group from others in the industry.

On the value of the program with regard to staff retention he has this to say: 'People overestimate the importance of what

Medium-sized business: aligning values and purpose

they get paid in the attraction and retention of staff. One of the worst things that can happen when you are running a business is losing good people, and losing the money that you have spent in the development and training of them. Most managers think it is about paying them as much as you can and selling them a dream around career promotion. That is certainly very relevant, but there needs to be more and different reasons why people would want to come to work with us at JC and why they would want to stay. I saw the work with our charity partners as offering something beyond salary—it has so much more meaning.'

One reason why the program has been implemented and embraced so strongly within the Jellis Craig Group is the commitment to do it right, for the right reasons. Nick sums it up well: 'It is rare in my opinion for people to move from wanting to do something to being able to do something or understanding what it takes to do it. We wanted to set up a vehicle that would make it easy for people to act. If we are able to create the opportunity for our people to help others, as is their desire, I am sure it will create a better workplace, and if they enjoy their workplace more then we will be more successful as a company. If they are happy they are not thinking about a career change, they are not thinking about moving. It also gives them more diversity and fulfilment in their lives.'

This is very much in line with the Optus strategy. Jellis Craig has around 350 staff, Optus closer to 9000, but Optus too saw part of its staff and community engagement strategy as 'enabling' staff and their families to connect with the community. It was very clear that one of Nick's reasons for creating the foundation was to act as an enabler. He saw the desire, he saw the heart and the willingness

> ... it's not the lack of desire or willingness, or even the lack of resources, but rather the structure or the *how* that is missing.

of his group to act, but they needed the structure to make it happen.

The experience that Nick identified in the team at Jellis Craig is not unique. Indeed I would suggest it is incredibly common within organisations of all sizes, and certainly within individuals. So often after delivering a keynote presentation I will have people walk up to me and say, 'I'd love to do what you have done, but I just don't know how'. So it's not the lack of desire or willingness, or even the lack of resources, I would suggest, but rather the structure or the *how* that is missing.

Building the foundation is one thing, and it is probably one of the easier steps in the process. Filling the positions on the committee to oversee the operation of the foundation was difficult only from the perspective of who to select and who to reject. The pool from which to draw was rich and deep, with talented people from across all areas of the business wanting to be involved. The challenge is keeping the energy alive not within the committee but among those outside who aren't attending the regular meetings. This is further evidence of the value of having a story to tell and creating a shared experience.

The benefits to the business have been immediate and beyond what might reasonably have been expected. Within months of launching the foundation Nick observed the changes: 'I am seeing a change not just in the work of the committee but in how positive they feel about life within Jellis Craig. It's not as if we were coming from a place with low morale and any slight improvement was going to be hugely visible. The group was a very positive place, but the differences even so early on are hugely visible.'

The focus by the Jellis Craig Group in building its CSR program was to concentrate on getting it right and telling the story internally first. This approach demonstrates the genuine desire to bring about change and to create the vehicle for such change. Rather than looking for the first available opportunity to champion their work to their external clients, Nick knows well that the benefits will come to the business in due course. 'What we are doing with the foundation will at some point filter outside the walls of Jellis Craig, and if that means people are more likely to list their property with us because they see us as good people, then that is fantastic.

'I do see that at some point in the future our doing good will also be good for business. I trust that will happen naturally. If it improves the success of our business then that will be another huge bonus, but it certainly wasn't the motivator for us starting this.'

Jellis Craig's approach to its CSR strategy is already creating benefits on both sides, for its charity partner and internally. Can it measure the success internally via hard evidence such as new listings or reduced turnover? Not yet, but as that was not the reason for embarking on this path, they are already winning. This is the essence of *doing good by doing good*.

I ask Nick to reflect on why it feels different now from what they have done in the past. 'It's obvious once you are doing it. It's the experiences we have already been able to tap into. It's what was missing in our previous attempts: from me and all the staff, there was a real lack of emotional commitment, and it's hard to drive a program of change without such a commitment, particularly when it is outside of the core business. Creating an experience is what brings it to life. The experience is the oxygen; it's not the money. The money is secondary, the money comes from that energy. We had it around the wrong way. We thought if we gave the money that would give us the experience. What we've learned is that you give the experience and the money will come.'

What advice would Nick give other businesses looking to establish their own CSR strategy? He thinks the following points are essential:

1   Have a diverse and engaged group to share the thinking, the strategy and the leg work, and allow others outside of the executive to take ownership.

2   Take your time and get the right people around you, equally distributed from across all areas of the business, to do the work.

3   Don't rush to promote the activities externally. Concentrate on promoting it internally and getting everyone on board, then the external promotion can and will occur in a more organic way.

4   Don't underestimate how hard it is to keep people on track and motivated. When it is not core business and involves hard work, their focus can certainly drift.

'We had it around the wrong way. We thought if we gave the money that would give us the experience. What we've learned is that you give the experience and the money will come.'

5   Focus on big visions but not big expectations. Take a long-term view and build it with patience. Don't expect to set the world on fire within the first 12 months and don't make it a one-year wonder.

6   Ensure succession is built into it from the word go. Recognise a need to develop champions within the business.

Narta: a focused, long-term commitment

On the face of it the combination seemed most improbable, and even today, for some, the relationship doesn't make obvious sense. A gathering of businesses with a combined buying power measured in *billions* come together to support a small (a very small) charity—and they live happily ever after with benefits flowing in both directions. For a charity founder, this may happen but once in their lifetime.

Narta, the National Associated Retail Traders of Australia, is a not-for-profit entity but, unlike many other models presented in this book, it is not raising money for charity and it's anything but a small entity when it comes to buying power. After almost 50 years of operation Narta has a combined buying power of $3.9 billion, which gives it 27 per cent of the Australian retail market. It is owned by the members and none of the earnings are retained, all being distributed back to the members every year.

Narta's role is technically to act as a conduit between members and suppliers to bring efficiencies to buying. Its member structure has changed dramatically over the past 15 years. Where it used to be dominated by the small, independent retailers, now it includes major corporations such as David Jones, Myer and JB Hi-Fi, but it still represents state-based members such as Bing Lee and offers many smaller retailers savings that they themselves would otherwise not be able to secure. Although the member base has changed over recent years with the addition of the big players, the essence of what Narta does remains the same—it pools its members' buying power in order to be competitive in the market. Previously its competition would have been other buying groups; now it is the bigger corporations.

Before 2007 Narta's contribution to the charity sector was a loose one based on patronage of its largest supplier and a feeling of expectation, rather than a connection on either a heart or a business level. It involved attendance at a couple of golf days but very little return to its member base. It ticked a few boxes and allowed it to point to the financial contribution to the group it was supporting and say, 'Yes we contribute to charity'. It was, in other words, your typical corporate philanthropy model, generating little interest or commitment of time or discussion by the executive team and no real investment in the outcomes of the contribution. The return matched the investment—very little. It had nothing to do with the amount of money it was contributing but everything to do with the lack of buy-in and the reasons behind the selection of the foundation it was supporting. It was seen as a necessary contribution rather than one based on free will and choice. As the CEO of Narta, Kay Spencer, comments, 'We were operating at arm's length and doing very little other than writing a cheque'.

It wasn't that Narta or the leadership team lacked the desire, will or heart to be part of something bigger, but the right fit hadn't come their way. They had explored workplace giving but realised that wouldn't offer the connection they were looking for. All that really did was shift or add to the contribution they were making on an organisational level. If giving from the member base didn't bring a lot of returns, they thought, why would pushing it down to the individual level change that? It wasn't the giving of the money or the amount that needed to change, they realised, but the entire model, which for them wasn't working.

> To be able to tell everyone of the difference they are making, to tell it with clarity and ideally with excitement, encourages others to get on board.

The change for Narta came when they were given a story. The outcome demonstrates the power and effectiveness of storytelling and why it's so important for charities, NFPs and indeed their corporate partners to have their own story. To be able to tell everyone of the difference they are making, to tell it with clarity and ideally with excitement, encourages others to get on board.

In 2007 Narta members gathered for their conference in the ballroom of the Four Seasons Hotel in San Francisco. There they heard the story of a very small charity that was doing something very ambitious but with a clear focus. They were introduced to an opportunity for the membership of Narta to make a real difference. So, in the most unlikely of places, an Australian speaker engaged to talk about leadership unknowingly presented the membership with the opportunity they had been looking for. What resonated so strongly with the group when they had actively been searching for an answer? Why did they find what they were looking for only when they stopped searching for it? Kay Spencer feels 'the catalyst was the fact that everyone was in the room. It was as if someone turned on the light switch, because everyone heard the same message, everybody felt the same empathy with the story and, more importantly, everyone thought, "This is a small boutique charity". This is an unknown factor but it is a good story'.

Without an ask from the stage, or even a suggestion of what their support might be able to do, the group came together as one. When the Narta leaders walked the room during the lunch break they gathered support to the tune of $250 000. With that single donation the charity was able to build a second home for the children of the tsunami in Thailand. That charity was, of course, Hands Across the Water.

The keys to the successful genesis of the unlikely relationship between Narta and Hands were as follows:

- There was a powerful story that the audience was able to connect with, in that every delegate in the room had personal knowledge of the events, having witnessed the devastation on their television screens.

- They weren't sold the charity. There wasn't even an ask, and at the time the project to build the home they would subsequently fund wasn't on the drawing board.

- The story had credibility, with evidence of work already done.

- There was a clear opportunity for them to make a difference.

- It was a new space with which they could connect for the appropriate reasons of doing good, rather than a pre-existing relationship or expectation.

- Their initial contribution underwrote the building of a new home, which satisfied the 'but for' test.

That initial contribution by the suppliers and members of Narta provided for a new home that would house 30 children in need, whose numbers had outgrown the original Hands home. Having achieved something quite remarkable and very tangible, Narta could have seen this as its model moving forward, so that every two years it would select a new charity partner and undertake a similar project. Instead it decided to stay with Hands, and indeed its commitment grew. What were its reasons for staying and how did it impact on the businesses?

'It galvanised the association,' Kay Spencer recalls, 'and it wasn't driven by Narta forcing it upon our members. It was our members and suppliers calling me up saying "we want to be part of this"'.

The charity also gave members of Narta the opportunity to be personally involved and part of the lives of the children they were now supporting. They got to spend time with them. They visited their homes and saw the very real difference they were making. In a global industry that knows well how to do the 'good life', Kay also sees a strong sense of 'perspective' in the group that previously wasn't there. But the interaction with those they are supporting isn't the only key to the success. Hands' 800 km bike rides through Thailand finish at the children's home, and a number of Narta members have participated in the ride, which has given them a shared experience. Such is the quality of this experience that Narta now runs an 800 km ride in Thailand just for its members, also finishing at the orphanage.

To extrapolate on the benefits of *doing good by doing good*, each of the Narta riders gets to share an experience over eight days with their colleagues, suppliers and competitors in an environment that is totally removed from the sometimes cut-throat world of business. They each enjoy the health benefits from training and participating in the epic ride and they spend eight days putting in extreme physical effort for someone else. The ride amplifies the benefits that their CEO sees in the relationship with the charity, including a new perspective, level of engagement and sense of purpose. And for every rider, of course, there are children whose lives are being transformed.

The Narta story is an example of what you often find in large business. They recognise the need to contribute back to the community and are willing to share profits, but they lack the engagement strategy or any return to them as a business. They need to have a charity partner or a philanthropic side to what they are doing, but it's not something they see the benefits from. Narta's previous giving wasn't part of the DNA of the business, and many staff would have struggled to articulate the change that was achieved through their involvement. The change in direction and the adoption of one main charity partner for the long term also shows the benefits both to the business and to the individuals within the business. In Narta's partnership with Hands it has been able to connect on a very deep and meaningful level. It has multiple touch points and a high level of engagement and participation.

Has the relationship between Hands and Narta remained on a typical donor/charity level, albeit a very productive and effective one? The answer is no. As the relationship between the two groups has strengthened over time, true shared value has flowed in both directions, made possible only through a unity of purpose that has built over time. Here are some of the outcomes that have been achieved that might not necessarily be part of your typical donor/charity relationship:

- The CEO of Narta, Kay Spencer, became so attached to the work of Hands after seeing the benefit to her industry and the change in the lives of the children that she resigned from an external board position and accepted a director's position on the board of Hands Across the Water, which she has held since 2008.

- Since 2010, Narta has been part of the annual Thai bike rides, which brings benefits to the riders, their businesses and of course to the charity.

- The daughter of one of the Narta team is on a 12-month placement at one of the Hands homes in Thailand, running the English-language training program.

- Through the Narta family one of the children from the tsunami project has undertaken a work placement on Hamilton Island.

- Narta holds its own 800 km, eight-day Thai bike ride that draws members and suppliers.

- Narta has funded the building of a small manufacturing complex at the tsunami project. The centre creates employment opportunities for the community, and training in manufacture, design and business. The products include corporate clothing, gifts and other items that Narta's members provide to their staff and customers. The supply of the goods brings a sustainable income source into the home and provides products that otherwise would have been purchased from a factory in China.

- Through direct Narta funding, each year six to ten children and their carers from one of the Hands homes in Thailand enjoy a sponsored trip to Australia and New Zealand, where they get to meet the staff and families of a number of the Narta family.

One of the best things to take from Narta's relationship with Hands is the object lesson of what can be done when a long-term commitment is made between two parties. Selecting one charity partner and committing to them brings with it challenges in disconnecting from others who are not part of the story, but the flip side is that the story allows for a level of deep engagement through shared experiences that wouldn't have presented if not for this long-term commitment. Maintaining just one charity partner for many years is not for everyone, but you can see the extended benefits that can occur should that be your chosen path.

When I ask Kay to reflect on the benefits that she has seen from the relationship she notes in particular:

- a strengthening of engagement within Narta's head office through the partnership with the charity
- a common denominator—something that all members and suppliers, regardless of their size, can be part of
- a shared common purpose that has galvanised the industry in relation to their giving

- the opportunity for members of Narta to be actively involved in the charity in many different ways—to have their own shared experience

- a deeper level of perspective.

The story of how Narta and Hands found their way into each other's lives is quite unique. From the experience I have gained in the charity sector over the past 10 years, such long-term relationships that provide so much value in both directions are few and far between. The success has been in the offering that the charity can deliver back to the donors, but a key to it is engaging the heart, soul and mind of those at the top. Without the support from the highest level to drive it through the industry it would have been very difficult, if not impossible. But what can the charity sector take from this relationship that has returned Hands well over $2 million in direct and indirect funding?

As a charity we need to be looking to add value for our partners. Give them a reason to engage, and more importantly give them reasons to belong and then to stay. No matter what industry we are working in we want loyal customers and supporters. We want our customers to become advocates for our brand and the work we do. To become advocates they need to believe, and to believe they need to have meaningful experiences. When the momentum shifts from external to internal, when those within the business start to take ownership and, as in the case of Hands, talk about the children as 'our kids' and about 'our homes', you have a partnership that is worth gold for all involved.

- The success of the partnership is not in the money contributed but in the alignment of values between the business and charity. Those values are best explored and communicated through shared experiences. Money provides benefits but that doesn't translate to engagement.

- The success of the partnership requires a champion to lead the way. Buy-in from the top is essential, but opportunities need to be created for those in the business to share in the journey in their own way. The greater the diversity of the opportunities, the greater the buy-in will be.

- More is achieved and more returned to the business by supporting fewer charities for longer.

- For both Jellis Craig and Narta it was never about a lack of heart, compassion or desire. What was missing was the alignment and shared experiences.

chapter 6

LARGE BUSINESS:
strategic investment

The two previous chapters have shown how small and medium-sized businesses can make a difference by addressing community needs (and benefiting the business in return) on a scale that might once have been considered the domain of large business.

The three cases studies that follow—of Optus, Unilever and TOMS—show how large business too can successfully adopt a very different approach from the old philanthropic model of donating cash. Optus shows how businesses can contribute in a huge way to community needs through their CSR programs without relying on straight cash injections. Unilever Global demonstrates integrated shared value and the serious intent of the company by attaching remuneration of its top executives to sustainability wins. TOMS embraces a very different business model, and is of a very different size from the other two companies, but is included in the big business group because of its scale and focus on a specific social need.

The other significant difference between the approach of small to medium business and the larger players in this space is that the larger corporates have found a way to effectively leverage and communicate the success of their programs. They also integrate the approach across a much broader reach of their operations and are able to commit greater resources to their programs.

Optus: an integrated shared value model

Optus is an Australian leader in communications and the digital field, providing services to more than 9.4 million customers every day. These customers are making an average of 240 million calls and sending 230 million SMS messages between them every week. To keep all of this happening Optus employs close to 9000 full-time employees.

In 2010 the Corporate Responsibility Steering Group was formed with a mandate to provide strategic leadership, governance and oversight and report directly to the Optus board. A focus of the Steering Group is to ensure its priorities are aligned with the business strategy of the company. Six members of the executive committee sit on the steering group, which indicates the significance of the role performed by the group.

The representation of the senior executive on the steering group and the influence that such a group brings highlight the value that Optus attaches to its sustainability commitments. It's hard to drive an agenda of change without an influential voice. The presence of the executive allows for such a voice.

The sustainability commitment sits across all areas of business and can be broken into four main areas. There is the influence over those who seek to work with Optus within the greater supply chain, those who are a part of Optus as either employees or end users, the company's environmental impact and its community programs. Bringing greater efficiencies into these core areas is good for business, which by default will be good for the community in which it operates. Optus has a responsibility to its shareholders to return a profit, and by focusing on initiatives that engage its stakeholders through responsible practices, it can achieve outcomes that are good for business and good for the community.

Optus recognises the value that can be derived for all its stakeholders from an increased focus on sustainability and it is now working to embed sustainability into leadership teams, ensuring key executive members own and advocate key sustainability initiatives.

Aligning key executives with sustainability initiatives or portfolios is a growing trend as companies realise the benefits of these programs need to be driven from the most senior of positions within the organisation. The 2013 'Your Voice' survey conducted by Optus reports that CSR is one of the top three drivers for employee engagement. No wonder there is an increased focus in this area.

In a good example of shared value, Optus imposes a set of standards to which suppliers looking to engage with them on projects must adhere. By imposing the standards on its suppliers, Optus recognises the opportunity to influence all of those involved in the supply chain of goods and services. It is in fact increasing its reach beyond what it does itself and bringing its suppliers and partners into the shared value model. The multiple layers of an integrated shared value model reaches along the entire supply chain. Through its Vendor Code of

Conduct it identifies the five key areas that must be covered by those looking to engage with it as suppliers. Those five key areas are corporate governance, occupational health and safety, environmental management, product stewardship and supplier management. Suppliers who can demonstrate that these five key areas are part of the way they do business are viewed more favourably in the selection process. The shared value model has many layers to it that when integrated are good for the community, the environment and the business.

With an eye on innovation, Optus continues to explore and embrace savings in the spend on power and reductions in the waste sent to landfill, as well as making positive contributions towards the health and welfare of its employees. All of these changes are good for both the community and the business.

> The shared value model has many layers to it that when integrated are good for the community, the environment and the business.

An increased focus on the health and welfare of its staff was signalled by the creation of the Health and Wellbeing Manager position in 2012, bringing increased access to services for employees. Improving the health of its teams results in reductions in sick leave and workplace injuries and increases the productivity of all. In the reporting year of 2013–14 it saw a tripling of the number of visits from employees to the Wellbeing site, showing a real take-up internally of the services offered by the Health and Wellbeing team.

A technology-based company will naturally continue to focus on innovation in the products it offers and access it creates but there is equal reward in vigorously pursuing the implementation of technology, systems or procedures that reduce the spend on consumables such as water and electricity. New technology implemented in its exchange centres has saved 9257 megawatt hours of electricity. Again, good for the environment, good for business.

The size of its motor vehicle fleet has been reduced from 572 vehicles in 2011–12 down to 392 in 2013–14, the last year of reporting, which saved more than 100 000 litres of fuel alone. The type and size of the vehicles has changed, and this too was seen in terms of a reduction in the spend on fuel. For each vehicle that is off the road the community benefits in multiple ways, including through the reduction in emissions and congestion and the increased use of public transport and healthier options such as cycling. The cost savings are not just to the company but to the community as well. Optus's contribution to the community in pure dollar terms through its community support initiatives such as direct cash funding, in-kind support, leverage, customer initiatives, staff time and workplace giving was reported to be $9.7 million for 2013–14. In 2014 Optus introduced yes4Good, a workplace giving program that increases from 13 to over 250 the number of charities where employees can choose to direct their contributions.

The thing with CSR reporting is that it enables you to represent economies as proactive steps by the company towards becoming better corporate and environmental citizens by supporting a reduction in waste and consumption. With a different spin, the same economies could very well be seen as pure cost savings introduced by the business to improve its financial position. In my time with the NSW Police the reductions we saw in the size of the vehicle fleet had nothing to do with reducing greenhouse gas emissions and everything to do with savings to meet an ever-reducing budget.

Reductions in waste or to the vehicle fleet may be driven by Optus's determination to reduce the environmental impact, or it may be creative reporting on internal cost-cutting. It's a bit like the TOMS story: which came first—the desire to provide shoes or to build a highly profitable company? The answer is it doesn't really matter. What was the primary driver of Optus in changing the vehicle fleet and the way it deals with waste? Again it doesn't really matter. The net result is its costs are reduced, which in turn makes it a more profitable company, and the community and environment benefit in a measurable way. All of which can legitimately be captured and form part of its annual CSR reporting.

Optus's focus on community investment aligns its business strategy and brand, which maximises the positive impact of the programs. 'You can't wrap your arms around everyone,' is how Helen Maisano, Optus's Associate Director of CSR, expresses it. Without a strong strategic approach, the community engagement of an organisation employing 9000 people could head off in many different directions.

The top-level strategic approach to community engagement for Optus is its commitment to vulnerable youth. Keeping to this broad compass enables it to engage on different levels, including education, improving employability, wellbeing and creating accessibility.

Its commitment to vulnerable youth makes good business sense as well as enabling it to make a real difference: youth are early adopters of and obviously a big market for technology-related products. Its commitment to the sector is not based on the traditional philanthropic approach of doling out chunks of money and then asking for a report at the end, hoping it hit the mark. While a financial commitment to those on the ground is very much part of what it does, its greatest leverage is gained through creating access to technology and people.

Its approach to community engagement is different from that of many other businesses represented in this book. It provides grants of up to $10 000—which in its last year of reporting amounted to $300 000, distributed to 38 community groups. But cash donations is not where its main energy is focused. In a unique approach, the team at Optus will look at a community problem or an initiative it feels it can add value to, and if there is an alignment with its values or business then it will lead the way forward. It will develop the framework and set the boundaries and then seek partners, who may be in the charity space or in the for-profit space, to help it achieve its goals.

An example of how Optus has recently brought together technology and its people to support an initiative is its work on the student2student program with its charity partner The Smith Family. The student2student program was aimed at addressing poor literacy standards in disadvantaged students. Optus' view is that the best way to address poverty in our community is to raise education standards, which in turn raises employment opportunities.

The program had previously been run using landline phones, with older children reading over the phone to the kids they were working with. Because of the limitations of the landline phone, the full potential of the program was not reached and participation rates decreased as the program continued.

Enter Optus. Through the injection of technology, capital and its people it was able to turn the program around. Switching from landline to mobile devices immediately expanded the reach of the program into rural areas that previously weren't involved. It also allowed for the program to take place outside the home. Kids were now reading to each other two to three times a week over an 18-week program as they went about their lives. This mobility took the success of the program to a much higher level. In the four years since the initial trial, the program has expanded from 50 to more than 500 student pairs. And Optus incentivised the kids by providing them with the handset and enough phone credit to get through the program. If they met the milestones along the way they received more credit, which they could then use for calling friends. At the same time the participants in the program were given an education in responsible phone use.

The results that were produced would allow even the harshest markers to declare the program a resounding success. Ninety-three per cent of participants improved their reading age relative to what it had been at the commencement of the program, over half improved it by one year and 40 per cent had increases greater than one year. If feedback from the participants and the families is anything to go by 99 per cent said they would recommend the student2student program to other families. Massive endorsement levels. As an added bonus, those who completed the program left with improved literacy standards and with a mobile phone that was theirs to keep. There was no requirement for them to remain part of the Optus network, but many of them did become customers. This was not the reason or driver behind the program, but it is an example of shared value at work.

When Optus looks to engage in a community program it sets conditions for their partners, just as it does for those who are part of the supply chain in the provision of services. But what it seeks in its charity partners is a little different from what it expects from its contractors working on the poles and cables.

> Optus wants to be sure that when the relationship has runs its course, the charity partner it has worked with is stronger than when they entered the relationship.

When Optus considers entering into a partnership with an NGO it seeks assurance that it is not creating a dependence. Optus wants to be sure that when the relationship has run its course, the charity partner it has worked with is stronger than when they entered the relationship. It is convinced that transactional or vendor-type relationships are not the ones that bring the value to them or, often, to anyone involved.

Optus's approach is reflected by that of Origin Energy, as profiled in chapter 7. It represents a change in corporate strategy on how large businesses engage with their charity partners. Rather than just giving away the money without any real vested interest in the return, corporates are increasingly asking questions about how change is going to be effected through their support.

While Optus's community engagement is clearly aligned to vulnerable youth, it recognises that many staff will have their own charity of choice and they are encouraged to support those causes that are close to their heart. Optus is not going to take their community engagement into the health sector or animal rights, for example, as there is no corporate alignment, but that doesn't mean it doesn't encourage its staff to follow the cause they believe in. It recognises the value of having staff who are committed to the community, even if it is outside the direction of the company. Here it sees its role as that of an enabler, assisting its people via matching grants or giving them time to participate.

Unilever Global: driving sustainability for business advantage

Unilever is a company that has embodied the principle of shared value in its approach to sustainability and growth. It repeatedly talks about the growth of the company matched by its investment in sustainable practices. Interestingly, though, it doesn't speak of corporate social responsibility or corporate philanthropy. As CEO Paul Polman puts it, 'We are finding out quite rapidly that to be successful long term we have to ask: what do we actually give to society to make it better? We've made it clear to the organisation that it's our business model, starting from the top'.

Unilever's Business Strategy opens with the following statement: 'In a world where temperatures are rising, water is scarce, energy is expensive, sanitation is poor in many areas and food supplies are uncertain and expensive, we have both a duty and an opportunity to address these issues in the way we do business.'

It alludes to the costs of resources but also the opportunities that exist. Right there is the success of shared value and integration within a business. Unilever sees the commercial opportunity and it sees the benefits to the society in which it operates. Which came first? Does it really matter, if both are achieved, what the initial motivator was? This is a theme that recurs throughout the book. The line between motivating force and impact becomes blurred. The cynic will see business change as driven first by profit and second by the opportunity to frame the direction of the business in a nice way. Certainly, without the very real potential for commercial return they wouldn't undertake these projects, but it is a win for business and a win for the community when both can be achieved.

Unilever has ambitious growth plans. In 2012 it established its Sustainable Living Plan. It recognises that putting sustainability at the heart of its business model not only secures its future but drives sustainable growth. The vision it has set itself is threefold:

> It recognises that putting sustainability at the heart of its business model not only secures its future but drives sustainable growth.

- to double the size of its business

- to reduce the size of its environmental footprint

- to increase its positive social impact.

What has been the impact on business since Unilever adopted this commitment to a sustainable future?

- It has seen sales increase from €40 billion to €51 billion in a four-year period, for an increase of 26 per cent.

- Its manufacturing eco-efficiency program has seen a reduction in costs of €312 million, which it calls its avoided costs.

- It has reduced its long-term supply risks by securing 36 per cent of its raw materials from sustainable sources.

In driving sustainability through the business, Unilever isn't pretending to be simply a good corporate citizen acting altruistically. It clearly articulates why its policy is also good for business. 'By reducing waste and material use, we create efficiencies and cut costs. This helps to improve our margins. By looking at product development, sourcing and manufacturing through a sustainability lens, opportunities for innovation open up. And we have found that by collaborating with partners including not-for-profit organisations, we gain valuable new market insights and extend channels to engage with consumers.'

Its position recognises that growth and sustainability aren't achieved at the expense of one another—quite the reverse. The 'virtuous circle of growth' is how Unilever likes to describe profit generation from its sustainable growth business model. The model shows the continual cycle of benefit that comes from sustainable living. Its investment in innovation and marketing will lead to profitable growth. Its reduction in waste also will contribute to their growth in the following ways:

- **Profitable volume growth.** Brands that are integrating sustainable living into their core purpose are driving success for the business. Unilever's range of sustainable products helps to drive growth with its retail partners.

- **Cost leverage and efficiency.** Unilever is creating efficiencies and cutting costs by reducing waste.

- **Innovation and marketing investment.** The company is looking at product development, sourcing and manufacturing through the lens of sustainability, which opens up opportunities for innovation and collaboration with external partners, including the not-for-profit sector.

Unilever has tied its horse to the innovation wagon, recognising that many commercial outcomes will be achieved by changing the way it does business. But it is also changing the way its business changes will occur. It is creating opportunities for external partners to share in the journey as it seeks the edge, and it is able to import into the company sustainability best practice by hand-picking the new partners it invites on board. At the retail end it is running joint-venture programs with retailers such as Tesco and Walmart, which conduct education programs on sustainable choices for their customers.

As with many of the corporates who have embraced the shared value model, Unilever sees innovation as a key to driving business into new markets and recognise that had it continued to operate under the previous paradigm then such opportunities would not have presented. Such is its attachment to the sustainable goals it is setting itself that the remuneration of a growing number of executives, including the CEO, is attached to the success of those goals.

> Unilever is creating opportunities for external partners to share in the journey…it is able to import into the company sustainability best practice by hand-picking the new partners it invites on board.

In 2012 Unilever launched its foundation to represent its 175 000 global workers. According to the 'Unilever Foundation: 2013 Update Report', 'The Unilever Foundation, together with our partners, has positively impacted the lives of more than 14.5 million people'. It has aligned itself with five international charities: Oxfam, UNICEF,

PSI (Population Services International), Save the Children and the World Food Program. The foundation rests on six pillars:

- global partnerships
- connecting with consumers
- advocacy
- disaster and emergency relief
- local program support
- employee engagement.

Unilever has made much of the importance of education, or 'reaching' vulnerable members of selected communities. There is a high incidence of education delivery attached to its programs, with public policy advocacy at the forefront of most of its partner relationships.

Unilever is not a company that is beyond criticism and I don't seek to promote it as the model of all things great in the corporate world. There will always be failings. Equally, even the organisation we hold up as representing best practice, by whatever measure, will draw critics. My position is not that Unilever, Optus or Origin cannot be faulted, but rather that by focusing as they do on shared value and innovation in the community space they are necessarily bringing improvements to the community in which they live and work, and creating benefits to the bottom line of their business at the same time.

TOMS: the genius of a simple model

The principle behind Blake Mycoskie's TOMS was to combine a for-profit with a social mission. Its success epitomises the concept of *doing good by doing good*.

The story behind the company begins when Mycoskie was travelling through Argentina and learned of a woman conducting a shoe drive to provide donated shoes to children for whom walking barefoot was the norm. As Mycoskie travelled around the country he became more aware of the problem and was inspired to support the cause. Struck by the limitations of this model, though, he thought a better approach would be to raise money to buy the shoes that could be donated to the children. That way he could overcome the problem of many of the children missing out on the donated shoes simply because they weren't in their size.

Then he hit on the idea of creating a for-profit business to help provide shoes for the children. 'Maybe the solution was the entrepreneurship, not the charity,' he thought, as he would later recall in his book *Start Something That Matters*. 'I'm going to start a shoe company that makes a new kind of alpargata. And for every pair I sell, I'm going to give a pair of new shoes to a child in need. There will be no percentages and no formulas.' One for one, it's as simple as you can get it. Each time someone buys a pair of shoes from TOMS, they donate a pair of shoes.

TOMS has been defined in many ways, including as 'a business model expressly built for purpose maximisation', as 'philanthropic capitalism' and as 'caring capitalism'. The challenge is in adequately describing an enterprise in which the lines between charity and for-profit are blurred, where the success of one relies intrinsically on the success of the other.

The success of the model is that it doesn't rely on donations, or the sympathy purchase; it relies on someone buying a quality, funky product for themselves, and every time they do a pair of shoes is donated to someone who, but for this donation, in all likelihood wouldn't have shoes. The genius of the model is its simplicity.

The program has expanded in many ways to improve the giving and outreach but continues to exemplify *doing good by doing good*. One of the tenets of creating shared value is that raw materials and manufacturing be located close to distribution. One benefit of this is that employment is generated within the local area. Increased employment opportunities benefit the local economy. It also reduces the cost of transporting materials across borders, and that has a saving in transport costs, use of consumable resources and emissions. Part of the TOMS vision is that by 2015 one-third of their shoes will be produced in the regions where they are given away.

> The challenge is in adequately describing an enterprise in which the lines between charity and for-profit are blurred, where the success of one relies intrinsically on the success of the other.

The program's fundamental purpose was to provide shoes for children who would otherwise go barefoot, but the giving of the shoes has created a pathway into the struggling communities that allows the provision of other resources such as microfinancing, health checks, screening to combat malnutrition and hookworm. As TOMS' giving has expanded so too have its retail offerings, which now includes eyewear and coffee, among an ever-expanding range.

None of this means the company or its philosophy is beyond criticism. It's hardly surprising that someone who has created a unique offering and done well for themselves financially should find that people are lining up to bring him down a peg or two.

One criticism of the model argues that Mycoskie has not brought an end to the problem of hookworm and that he would be better off building concrete toilets to combat the disease rather than giving shoes that offer only a temporary barrier to the worm, which lives in fecal matter. The implication is that he should give a portion of his profits to building toilets throughout the developing world, which would be a worthy alternative but misses the key that a massive part of his success has been tapping into a culture—a generation of people who by buying a pair of shoes feel they are contributing, and but for the direct correlation and the simplicity they might very well choose to buy another pair of shoes that produces no benefit to charity. He is not curing the root cause of the problem, but who said that was his mission or that *should* be his purpose?

The second criticism, which to my mind is more persuasive, is that by conducting his shoe drops and unloading thousands of pairs of shoes in an area he may be putting any local manufacturer out of business. This criticism could be overcome by shifting his manufacturing operations to the country in which he is delivering the shoes. The benefits of employment and the supply of raw materials will remain in the local community, even if the profits return to TOMS and Mycoskie in California.

Here's what makes TOMS work:

- The shoes are funky!

- The business model is sustainable.

- It gives people a story and it says something about their identity. Your customers then become your storytellers and your supporters. They buy the shoes for the story so they're happy to be attached to it, and more importantly to share that story with potential new customers.

- The process of ordering the shoes online is painless.

- The cost of the shoes is comparable to what you would expect to pay, ignoring the charity aspect to the model.

Customers with a social conscience know what is happening at the other end. There is no vague 'a percentage of this goes to communities in need', the kind of statement that feels more like a marketing gimmick than a genuine attempt to share the profits. 'What percentage, what community and what is that support?' Buying a pair of TOMS, you know what is happening at the other end. And this is good for business — actually it's *great* for business. In the first five years of operation the company gave away more than one million pairs of shoes, which means it sold one million pairs of shoes, at a retail price of US$40 a pair. It's not hard to do the maths; $40 million in the first five years of business is a good turnover by any measure. TOMS recently celebrated giving away its 10 millionth pair of shoes.

It's also great for the communities TOMS supports. The more successful the company is, the greater their giving. Wouldn't it be great if you could articulate the philanthropic position of your company with such clarity, with no messy formulas, so it is instantly believable?

- The bigger the business, it sometimes seems, the bigger its claims of addressing community needs, yet in reality these grand claims often reflect a lower level of support as a percentage of revenue.

- Larger businesses, through increased resource tolerance, have a greater capacity to commit to projects by way of partnering with experts.

- Among larger businesses there is a greater focus on the 'benefits to the community' through their reduction in consumption of power, water and other finite resources. By reducing their spend on these resources they are able to bring direct savings to their operations.

- Innovation leads to new markets and new opportunities. Large corporates have the tolerance to invest in R&D in pursuing what otherwise might have been unattractive opportunities, and in so doing create new markets and innovative change to their business offerings.

chapter 7

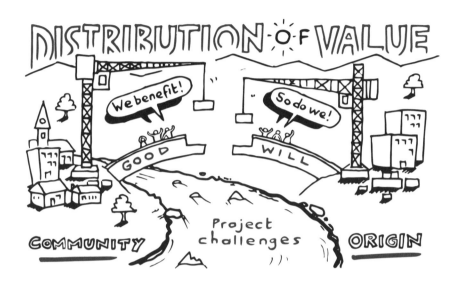

THE ORIGIN STORY

Origin Energy is Australia's leading energy retailer, employing more than 6000 employees across the country. A top 20 ASX-listed company, Origin is involved in gas exploration and production as well as power generation and energy retailing. It has over 4.3 million customer accounts and in partnership with Australia Pacific LNG (APLNG) is developing Australia's largest coal seam gas to liquefied natural gas project.

As a company involved in the exploration and harvesting of gas reserves it is accountable to multiple stakeholders. As a publicly listed company it is accountable to 160 000-plus shareholders, who expect it to return a profit each year and to grow the share price. It is also accountable to the communities in which it operates, the customers it serves, its employees and of course to the various regulators who sit across its industry.

The relationships it needs to have with stakeholders in the gas fields are unique to the extraction industry. It will enter a community with a view to conducting exploration for gas reserves. This may see it establish a presence in that community, typically for two to five years. If it finds adequate reserves the required approval process may take several more years before extraction begins. Its full tenure within a community can be up to 40 years, although the average is closer to 20 to 30 years. Depending on how the relationship is managed it may be deemed a welcome guest and a valued member of the community or, in some instances, tolerated as an unwelcome visitor whose departure cannot come quickly enough.

> It cannot afford to behave arrogantly or without authenticity, because it needs to have the support of this community — and the next and the one after that.

The management of these relationships is therefore crucial, which is why CSR, community engagement and shared value are so important for Origin. It cannot afford to get it wrong. It cannot afford to behave arrogantly or without authenticity, because it needs to have the support of this community—and the next and the one after that. It needs the backing of those it is working with, but at the same time it must satisfy the interests of its shareholders, who are looking for a maximum return on their investment on every project.

Shared value at work—the Origin way

Origin has been involved in working with multiple partners successfully for many years. It has two clear lines to its CSR platform: the first is sustainability, which includes its environmental stewardship and the socioeconomic view that it takes to working with its community partners; and the second is the Origin Foundation, which is the philanthropic arm of the business.

Origin's sustainability approach is a great example of shared value at work, although it calls it *distribution of value* and was operating in this way long before the term 'shared value' first came out of Harvard Business School.

The Origin Foundation was formed in 2010 and is more closely aligned to the typical corporate philanthropic model of supporting community projects through the injection of funds, matching grants, sponsoring staff via volunteering days and pro-bono support.

In the true sense of the concept of shared value, Origin understands that for continued success it is in its interest to deliver value to the communities in which they work. Raj Aseervatham, the General Manager of Sustainable Development and Communities, sums it up like this: 'For us to be successful tomorrow, our stakeholders must want us there'. It is in the business interests of Origin to ensure the communities in which it operates prosper as a result of its presence. It has a duty of care to manage any impacts of its activities and to ensure it is

> In the true sense of the concept of shared value, Origin understands that for continued success it is in its interest to deliver value to the communities in which it works.

delivering value while it is there, and indeed to ensure that this value continues long after its departure from the community. It is committed to building capacity within the communities and for that capacity to have strong elements of sustainability and distribution of value.

Part of the concept of shared value as proposed by Michael Porter and Mark Kramer is the idea of *clustering*, whereby local communities are built to provide the skills and services that otherwise would see products transported to allow for the next stage of production. If Origin can't find the resources and skills locally it needs to import them. Conversely, goods are normally transported along the supply chain to add value in the manufacturing process, but in the extraction industry they need to bring the resources to them.

The situation

For its gas extraction work Origin will often establish operations in remote country areas or undeveloped international locations. Depending on their success such projects may last anything up to 40 years, so the demand for people to build and run the facilities provides both a challenge and an opportunity.

Typically the small rural towns that Origin operates in or close to find it difficult to retain their young people. Employment opportunities may be limited to the family farm or business. The towns aren't often blessed with further education options such as universities or colleges, and many school leavers will leave the community where they grew up to head for the city.

As those finishing school leave the area it creates a void in the community. Even those who had planned to return with a degree in four years' time may have found employment elsewhere in a community that offers them the social and community infrastructure they need. The upshot is communities in regional Australia that are missing generations. Typically the older generation remains, as do those who have younger children at school, if there is a school in the community, but those aged 17 to 25 have mostly left to seek further education and employment and few will return.

Origin finds on entering these communities that local businesses often are not familiar with the engagement process—contracting conditions, health, safety and environmental standards and so on—for such large operations. The local metal works, engineering workshop or mechanic may very well have the technical skills required and be capable of performing the work, but the process of winning the work for such large projects can be foreign to them, and it is this inexperience, rather than a lack of skills, that can stand in their way.

The challenge

Companies such as Origin face a range of such challenges on entering these communities. Here is Sue Horn, Senior Manager of Regional Development for Origin:
'Entering the communities there will be various preconceptions and expectations from the community. Some might expect there will be a windfall in new jobs immediately, but that is not normally the case in the construction of the plant. There will be immediate benefits to the community but not necessarily involved in the construction stage.

Part of the challenge is building the capacity of the local businesses to meet the increased demand and successfully compete for the new business that is coming to their town.

We need to address those expectations right from the beginning and we do that with communication sessions that are very transparent and, we have found, appreciated by the community.'

The benefits to the community of any new industry moving into rural Australia can be felt immediately. From the local service station to the pie shop feeding the workers, to the motels, the pubs—all businesses providing goods and services are likely to see an increase in demand with the rise in population. Part of the challenge is building the capacity of the local businesses to meet the increased demand and successfully compete for the new business that is coming to their town. Often they will manage well enough at the start but find it more difficult to compete sustainably as the operation and demand continue to grow.

Many of the local providers will previously have won business based on one of two reasons: either they have the relationships in the town or they are the sole provider of the services. All that changes when an organisation such as Origin comes to town and the requirements around OH&S, the environment, compliance and the ability to demonstrate their technical competence must be satisfied.

A second, more long-term issue is one around employment opportunities for school-leavers. Every small country town in Australia faces the problem of retaining school-leavers and providing employment opportunities for those who would stay.

How does a company such as Origin move into these remote towns and find the infrastructure it will need for up to 40 years to enable it to operate successfully? Without existing infrastructure it needs to bring it in with it. The resources industry has perfected the mobile workforce, moving people into remote sites using a fly-in, fly-out (FIFO) strategy. Hundreds of workers on a rotating basis will be flown into a site, housed in temporary accommodation at the mine site and then, a week or two later, flown out and replaced by another crew. This continues for as long as the operation remains viable. This approach was born of necessity, but often it is not a sustainable solution as it denies opportunities to the local communities.

The opportunity

When Origin arrives in a community there will be technical skills and expertise it will need to bring with it. But there are also many roles that, given appropriate training, the local community can fill. Training the local community brings benefits to both Origin and the community (see figure 7.1).

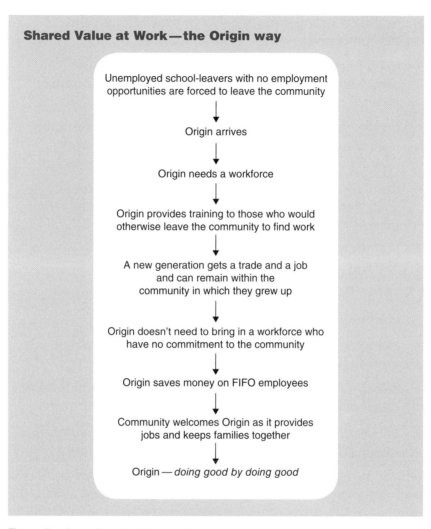

Figure 7.1: how shared value contributes to the success of the community and the company

Community benefits include:

- increased employment opportunities across a range of areas that wouldn't exist but for the increased population brought into the town

- up-skilling of the community, which increases their capabilities and employability beyond the work with Origin

- training that provides a skill for life and is transferrable at any time to any location

- forging a stronger partnership between Origin and the community
- reducing the need for school-leavers to leave their community, thereby keeping families and communities intact
- greater commercial opportunities within the community with increased demand for goods and services both directly and indirectly related to the activities of Origin
- through training and retaining school-leavers, creating a workforce made up of local community members, rather than FIFO
- building economically stronger communities.

Benefits for Origin include:

- closer relationships with the community, which encourages harmonious coexistence
- reduced costs for transporting and accommodating large outside workforces
- increased reliability of the supply chain on a local level as a result of the training it brings
- the creation of a stable local workforce who are supported by the families living within their own community.

Origin brings immediate and longer term benefits to the communities it enters, but it is not a task it takes on alone. In a number of the communities it has found that local contractors have embraced the opportunity of entering the supply chain at various points, but have lacked the capacity to clearly articulate their business offering or to meet various levels of compliance. Often there is not a major gap in what is required to help the local contractors increase their capacity to meet the requirements and clearly articulate their business.

Origin has formed a number of joint-venture partnerships with state and local government and industry groups to offer training and capacity-building for contractors. It might be as simple as helping the local contractors articulate their business offering. The benefit of this is twofold. First, it enables the larger contractors in the supply chain who are working directly with Origin to assess and select the local contractors with confidence. Second, it helps the local contractor clarify what they are offering as a business, and this may identify opportunities they previously hadn't recognised. This capacity-building in conjunction with external partners brings returns to the community and to Origin, which can then ensure its contractors along the entire supply chain are fit for purpose and compliant with operational requirements and safety regulations.

Assessing and addressing community needs

Origin starts each project with an assessment of the community's needs with a view to the distribution of value, and it does this before it even enters a community. Its starting point is to ensure the rights and interests of the community are protected and any negative impact is mitigated. Following the community needs and resources assessment it undertakes a socioeconomic analysis of the community, establishing a baseline of what services currently exist, what might be needed and the best way to close the gap between the two. As part of its early work it will look at access to schools and health care, what gaps exist in training and what community needs can be filled with the most impact.

> Its starting point is to ensure the rights and interests of the community are protected and any negative impact is mitigated.

With the benefits of insights from a socioeconomic baseline it then consults with the community to determine what the community sees as its needs and how a partnership can be built between the two. It might sit down with the community and say, 'We have conducted a review of the community and looked at current access to services and resources and what you might need, we believe we can add value in the following ways ... What do you see as your greatest needs as a community?'. The aim is to provide resources that bring compounding value to the community. For example, providing entrepreneurial training for women, something often lacking in country towns, creates a long-lasting benefit for the community.

The greatest benefit that Origin takes from meeting the needs of the community is building goodwill between the various stakeholders involved in every project. As Raj Aseervatham notes, 'Each of our projects will face challenges at some point in their life. If we have worked together with the community from day one, if we have invested in building that goodwill, it enables us to deal with the challenges as they arise in a conciliatory approach rather than problems escalating'.

Ostwald Bros — a contracting partner

The story of the construction and mining services company Ostwald Bros is one of sustained growth, much of which can be attributed to investment in the local community. Among other ventures, the company delivers large-scale infrastructure work for regional developments and resource sector projects. Its vision is to be a preferred contract partner for resource and infrastructure clients Australia-wide. As a tier 2 company, it likes to think of itself as a 'big small company' that remains true to its values from its humble beginnings. It is a contracting partner to tier 1 companies such as Origin. Brendan Ostwald, the founding principal and now CEO of the business, recognised early on the benefits of investing in the local community. 'We need to have a fly-in, fly-out capacity as part of our toolkit and offering. We simply can't develop all of the skills that we might require for every project from the local community. But what I am clear about is that investment in training in the local community, who might otherwise not get the type of benefits they now receive, is both good for us as a company and good for the community.'

Ostwald has seen how investing in the local community also brings stability to the workforce and it enjoys unprecedented retention rates based on the investment it has made in its people and in addressing a community need. 'We have Gen Y, who now have long-service leave. Those two statements are just not heard in the one sentence,' says Ostwald.

The benefits to the community compound when you are able to offer stability and long-term security and far outweigh the initial investment in the training. 'We made a massive investment in the training of our guys at the front end of the process and that training certainly continues, but we see the benefits to the community above importing workers who leave as soon as their rotation is over. We see the emergence of sporting clubs, and we see families who add so much to the community and breathe life into these rural areas. I know that our business benefits and I also know the community is benefiting on multiple levels from our investment in the training of those who might otherwise be unemployed or leave the community in search of work. What we are also giving them are skills for life. Their skills are transferable should they choose to move on.'

While Ostwald Bros embraces a CSR program that provides scholarships for students of civil engineering, the biggest impact it is making is through its shared value model of clustering. Investment in the local community via its commitment to training and employing locally allows those benefits to be shared across communities, which will have long-term benefits. Acknowledging the benefits to the business of high retention and engagement rates, it too is benefiting directly from its investment in the community.

Without setting out to address a specific societal need directly, as do some of the larger companies profiled in the book, Ostwald Bros demonstrates that the same shared value benefits can be created in different ways.

Constraints on measuring and reporting

Origin is a member of the LBG (formerly London Benchmarking Group), which is discussed in greater detail in chapter 10. The reporting takes a number of formats. Each year it produces a Sustainability Report, which is publicly available and subject to review. The sustainability claims made in the report are independently audited. To complement that report a social and environmental report is produced every six months by APLNG.

Origin acknowledges in its reporting that the environmental impact is much easier to measure than the social impact of its presence. It is far easier to measure, validate and report on the number of megalitres of water that was diverted from rivers to farmland than it is to analyse and quantify the benefits of investing in training of youth who might otherwise have left the community to look for work in other areas.

Origin can measure and report on the cost of the training, the number of courses run, the number of participants involved in the training; it can even report on the improved education standards of those who participated. But how does it measure the ongoing or compounding social and economic benefit of that training? Here Origin's difficulty is no different from that experienced, for example, by Optus in its student2student program. The inputs and outcomes are identifiable, but the true value sometimes resists statistical measurement.

The Origin Foundation

The second part of Origin's CSR model operates more in line with a traditional corporate foundation, except they approach it rather differently. Its focus is on education and it looks to support organisations who are working to bring about longer term change. The Origin Foundation was established in 2010 with a corpus of $50 million. The income from the investment of the corpus is used to fund its philanthropic activities. Sean Barrett, the head of the Origin Foundation, reported that in the financial year 2013–14 the investment of the corpus returned approximately $3 million for the foundation to use in its philanthropic activities. The operating costs of the foundation are underwritten by Origin, which ensures the total return on the investment is put into its activities.

The foundation is a relatively new concept for Origin and the decision to support education as its main theme was made by the employees of the company. When setting up the foundation Origin was very keen to ensure it was supporting the will of the people within the company and not the vision of a select few.

The commitment to its charity partners is not confined to the distribution of the income derived from the investment of the corpus. While offering the more traditional volunteering option, it also understands the value of skilled volunteering. It gives its employees the opportunity of volunteering their business skills to work on building capacity and sustainability within its charity partners. A total of 5500 hours of volunteering was contributed in 2013, with 25 per cent of that skilled volunteering. Sean Barrett sees this as a real growth area within the Origin team and one that is of the greatest value to the charities it is supporting. Encouraging skilled volunteering is very much in line with the longer term approach the foundation takes to its corporate philanthropy.

Sean Barrett indicates that over 75 per cent of its grants to charities are above $100 000. This is in stark contrast to the current trend among corporate and philanthropic foundations. The Centre for Social Impact reported in its paper 'Where the Money Goes' (July 2013) that 80 per cent of grants by corporate and philanthropic foundations are of less than $50 000.

Again unlike a lot of corporate foundations, Origin doesn't call for grant submissions from the charity sector. Like Optus, it identifies a need in the education area and then looks for charity partners it can work with to address that need. After the necessary due diligence is carried out, and if there is alignment between values and desired outcomes, Origin will enter into a multi-year relationship with its partners. The relationship is not one based on funding without support, though. Particularly in the early days, it seeks to ensure the charity partners have what they need to bring about change and realise their goals.

Sean Barrett is particularly keen to emphasise that the foundation doesn't look to interfere, but rather to ensure the program has the greatest chance of success. 'If that means injecting skilled volunteers or even more cash into the project we would do so,' he says, but understanding the needs can only come about through remaining connected and part of the program. 'One of the things we are aware of is in granting the money there is a real imbalance of power. Some view those who have all the cash as having all the power. We want to remove that imbalance and work in partnership with our charities.'

On measuring and reporting the impact of these programs, Origin experiences the same sorts of difficulties as many other social initiatives, indeed not dissimilar to those it encounters in its sustainability projects. Again, measuring resource inputs and outcomes is relatively easy, but measuring the overall social impact on the communities it is assisting is more complex, as is measuring the return to the business through increased engagement and staff retention, for example. Origin points out that its investment in community programs extends over several years, and to reach any conclusions so soon after the formation of the foundation and the implementation of the partnerships would be premature.

'Some view those who have all the cash as having all the power. We want to remove that imbalance and work in partnership with our charities.'

The Origin Foundation looks to measure its commitment to the sector in three main ways:

1   **Foundation effectiveness.** This involves an assessment
    of the performance of the foundation itself against
    the measures of good governance and investment
    performance, an independent assessment of the
    performance of the board, and an in-depth survey of its
    partners to measure its effectiveness.

2   **Proxy measures.** The people and organisations who receive grants are assessed to gauge the level of value that has been added by the foundation. The goal is to build capacity within its partners to ensure that at the end of the relationship they are stronger as an entity than they were when they entered the partnership.

3   **Beneficiaries measures.** What are the outcomes or outputs that have been achieved by the receivers of the support, and what difference has the support made to them?

Measuring the return to the internal stakeholders of the business is something Origin would like to do more effectively than it is right now, but again, given that the foundation is still in its infancy, those measures are more likely to present in the coming years.

Sean Barrett has no doubts about the returns to those involved in the skilled volunteering undertaken as part of the CSR strategy. 'What I have seen is a huge benefit to those who have been involved and have had their own personal experience. Particularly for those who are working in the finance area of Origin. For them to go out into the community and inject their skills into some of the organisations that would never have had access to such talent is hugely rewarding for these guys. It brings enormous value to the not-for-profit, and the guys walk away with a real endorsement of their skills and the value they have provided. It also gives them a sense of perspective on the challenges we face in our lives.'

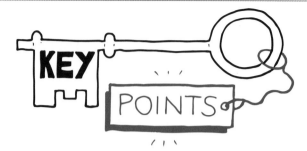

The Origin case study provides a number of examples of how different approaches to engaging the community can and do bring benefits to all involved:

- Companies have the opportunity to engage with the community, but they have a responsibility to their shareholders to ensure that their community investment programs are providing value back to the company.

- Investment in longer term strategies are more likely to return benefits to the community that are sustainable and build capacity. The way in which the relationship is built with one community will contribute to the relationships that are built with successive communities.

- The *distribution of value* model, which is an integral part of Origin's engagement strategy, focuses on building long-term sustainable capacity within its partners.

- Community engagement programs are enhanced by a consultative approach, and when stakeholders who have an interest are invited to be part of the program.

chapter 8

CHARITY
TAKING
THE LEAD

What role does the not-for-profit sector have to play in the conversation around CSR, which is, after all, concerned with *corporate* social responsibility.

This chapter is not about the charity partners thinking they can teach their donors or supporters how to suck eggs. It's about charities taking responsibility for the relationship with their existing or future donors and recognising what makes for a successful relationship. There can be a sense of entitlement within the charity sector, a belief that corporations should be supporting them, that because they are 'doing the work that others won't' a different set of rules should apply to them. Josephine Sukkar, principal at Buildcorp and a director of NFP boards, believes 'it is incumbent upon the corporate world when undertaking business development through events and the like that they create fundraising opportunities for charities as part of those events', but this doesn't mean we as charities don't need to work for your dollars.

Relying on grant applications is in itself a limiting strategy for charity fundraising. Charities need to offer more in return for the dollar, be that an experience or a product. Untied large grants are becoming less the norm. Optus's community and sustainability focus in 2014 saw it commit $9.7 million; of that, $300000 was in grants, with 38 grants capped at $10000 awarded. If charities want to engage their corporate and business partners, they are going to need to do more than just ask for money.

The significance that businesses operating in this space place on the role of the charity or NFP will depend on their level of maturity and position on the CSR participation continuum. Those companies who each year carve off a portion of their earnings, savings or staff donations to make a one-off charitable donation, I would suggest, leave the charities with little to do other than to say 'thank you'. These are the companies who often change charity partners each year or have a multitude of partners but lack either the level of interest or the capacity for a deeper relationship.

Companies a lot further along the continuum see their chosen charities as true partners who are key to the formation of the strategy. The partners will work together to address key specific community needs, or at the least will be in frequent communication with each other during the term of the relationship.

So which is the best type of relationship for the charity or NFP entity, and where should they be expending their energy?

Strategic development

Charities need to invest time in strategic development and not become complacent by relying on the idea that people will give to them simply 'because they are a charity'. The charity space is incredibly crowded and the fact that you are saving children's lives, finding a cure for cancer, protecting whales or feeding the homeless is nice, but it's not enough.

Most charities are doing good, or at the very least were established to do good. They all have a compelling story, but every day corporations hear compelling stories from charities who want a piece of their pie. The differentiator is not what you do as a charity or how well you do it; it is who can best articulate the returns to their donors that will win the prize.

An effective part of a charity's strategic development is knowing who they do and don't want to partner with, and when to say no to money. For meaningful outcomes there has to be authenticity on both sides of the ledger. Individuals and businesses see the value of attaching themselves to charity—they like what that says about them. Have you noticed the growing number of 'philanthropists' out there? In my book, participating in a charity bike ride doesn't make you a philanthropist. Paying for the guy in the car behind you at the McDonald's drive-through, and then telling the world about it on Facebook, doesn't make you a philanthropist—it makes you a tool! Can we introduce a rule that says you need to give away a minimum of $1 million a year, from your own personal wealth, before you can call yourself a philanthropist?

> The differentiator is not what you do as a charity or how well you do it; it is who can best articulate the returns to their donors who will win the prize.

Then there are the businesses who talk about the charity they support, without a story about the specific program or the difference made. Dropping $50 once a year into the Salvos appeal doesn't give you legitimacy as a 'corporate partner of the Salvation Army'.

Charities need to be responsible for their brand just as much as the corporate or business. The larger charities have worked it out that if you want to include their symbol on your email footer it will come at a price. Businesses are doing it to buy themselves goodwill and it's only right that there be a price attached to that.

In setting the strategy for the overall relationship between donor and charity partner, or even for an individual project, time should be invested in answering a number of questions:

- What is the overall objective of the project?
- What resources (inputs) are required?
- What will be produced (outputs) during the project?
- What difference will we make (impact)?
- Is there a clear conclusion to the project?
- How will we communicate the results of the project?
- How will we measure the success of the project?
- What are we benchmarking the success against?

Charity groups that can lead their business partners or donors down this path demonstrate that they are committed to the success of the program, are invested in seeing their donors achieve the best outcome and are responsible business partners. This type of approach will also give confidence to new partners that the charity group is progressive and likely to be using funds to secure the best outcomes by committing itself to such transparency around results.

It's a crowded marketplace

Estimates vary, but sources such as the Australian Taxation Office and the Australian Charities and Not-for-profits Commission (ACNC) suggest there are currently around 600 000 NFP or charity organisations in Australia. This number includes the large, widely recognised and supported charities such as the Salvation Army, Red Cross, Oxfam, The Smith Family and a host of cancer-related charities. It also includes your footy club, the seniors tennis club and even perhaps the local lapidary club, along with myriad causes and community collectives whose charitable objectives will vary vastly in focus and ambition.

A common feature of these very different community groups is some type of formal structure whose purpose is *not* to create profit, so you can bank on it that close to 600 000 of them will spend a good part of their time focused on raising money.

The ACNC, which was introduced in the Australian 2011 federal budget and began operations on 3 December 2012, was established to serve as the central regulator representing the charity and NFP sector and to harmonise the state-based fundraising laws. Just over 10 per cent of charities and NFPs are ACNC-registered. The ACNC has three categories for those undertaking fundraising based on revenue:

- small charity—annual revenue is less than $250 000
- medium charity—annual revenue is $250 000 or more, but less than $1 million
- large charity—annual revenue is $1 million or more.

The first time I saw these figures I was surprised by the number of charities raising less than $1 million a year, which seemed low as a cut-off between the medium and large charity categories. I was of course viewing it through the lens of my experience with Hands Across the Water, which was raising well over a million dollars a year, yet when I discussed Hands it was always as a 'small or boutique charity'. We operate without premises, and until early 2014 we had the equivalent of half a full-time paid employee. Not what I would consider large, or even medium. What this illustrates is the modest size of so many of the organisations and community groups that are out there having a go.

Make it easier to say yes

So what is the appetite and approach of the charity groups towards CSR? We talk about the positioning of corporations or business on the CSR participation continuum and we could easily overlay the charity groups to find where they sit on the same continuum to gauge their interest in CSR.

The small charities or community groups (according to the ACNC model) raising less than $250 000 a year aren't going to be involved in deep relationships with corporate partners. Their revenue will come from lots of small activities and potentially one 'major' event during the year, which might be a dinner or experience-based event.

The medium-sized charities raising up to $1 million a year, particularly those pushing towards the top, will have sound recurrent funding and longer lasting relationships with business or corporate partners. They have a solid, reliable income-generating model and operate in a more strategic role than those generating less than $250000 a year. Medium-sized charities will certainly have reason to focus on building mutually beneficial relationships with their partners, if they don't already have them.

Those charities consistently generating more than $1 million a year will have entrenched corporate partners. The larger charities that push into the tens of millions of dollars a year will have teams dedicated to managing those relationships.

But does all of this mean that the domain of the CSR beneficiaries rests only with the larger charities? The answer is a very definite *no*.

Looking at how small businesses such as WordStorm and Churchill Education have entered the CSR space and how important it has become for them, there is no reason to expect that other charities of a similar size can't benefit. In fact, smaller businesses need smaller charities to partner with. I have heard many a story of business groups looking to downsize their charity partners because of the lack of love they are shown or the absence of engagement they feel when working with larger partners.

A $50000 donation by a small company can represent its total commitment and a huge amount of work on its part. A donation of that size could cover a small charity's annual operating expenses; for a large charity it would be just one of many large donations it receives each month.

> There is space for charities of all sizes to work more closely with their partners and sponsors to bring mutually beneficial rewards.

There is space for charities of all sizes to work more closely with their partners and sponsors to bring mutually beneficial rewards. Charities that remain passive in their engagement and partner relationship strategies limit their potential to build revenue and therefore limit the services they can offer. Much like the business that simply hands over a cash donation each year, they are restricting their return on investment.

In chapter 11 we look at how those shared experiences bring deep engagement to those involved; in chapters 6 and 7 we considered the different levels of corporate engagement with charity and compared these models. But what if the charities went beyond creating opportunities for engagement to identify and then lead the way for business to create the shared value that brings positive returns?

If charity groups, large and small, can lead the way for the business partners to benefit from their contribution to the sector, then that will give them more reason to invest—and the proverbial pie increases in size.

How does charity take the lead on this?

The idea of creating positive business returns for their partners, when they are always looking to find ways to feed themselves, can be quite foreign to small and medium-sized charities and even some of the larger ones. But for many the magic already lies within what they do. No change in direction or focus is required; they need only increase their awareness of what they've got to offer.

Let me give you two examples of how easily this can play out.

In the first example, the representative of a charity turns up to pitch to a new corporate partner. They are seeking a donation of $25 000. In their pitch they will typically talk about:

- why they need $25 000
- what difference the money will make
- what they have done in the past
- how worthy and good they are
- how little they spend on fundraising (if it's a lot they will leave this one out)

- how, in return for the $25 000, they will display the logo of the business at an event
- how they will provide a newsletter reporting the success of the program.

The hour is over, the pitch is complete, and the charity leader walks away knowing they have given the potential partner a deeper insight into what they are about and what they will do with the money. They will also leave behind a glossy brochure and will exchange business cards.

It could be that the meeting and the pitch are *exactly* what the potential donor was looking for. But the fundamental question here is what is in it for the donor? What do they take from that hour-long meeting other than a deeper insight into what the charity does? How will *their* business benefit from engaging with the charity? The answer to the last question won't come from the meeting; it will be for the business to determine that for themselves.

> The fundamental question here is what is in it for the donor?

In the second example, the charity partner turns up with exactly the same brief but presents it in a very different way:

- The work we do connects to your vision and values in these three ways:

  1 ....
  2 ....
  3 ....

- By partnering with us on this event these are our core objectives, the outcomes and impact we expect to achieve:

  1 ....
  2 ....
  3 ....

- Here is a copy of our marketing and communication plan for the event and the life of the project.
- Without your support this project will not proceed.

- We will create opportunities for your staff and their families to be involved in the program in the following ways:

  1 ....

  2 ....

  3 ....

- As a key partner we will offer your team these opportunities, above and beyond those offered to the other supporters who will be present:

  1 ....

  2 ....

  3 ....

- We are holding an event to launch the project and we expect to attract 500 people on the day and reach another 10 000 via our online campaign. Here is the breakdown of the demographic of those we reach.

- This is the list of businesses who will be involved/present that are aligned to your area.

- This is the strategy that we have in place to report back to you the exposure your brand has received by partnering with us on this project.

With the same brief we have given to the potential donor clarity around the project and how essential their support is; opportunities for a shared experience involving their team and their families; alignment of values; business development opportunities; and a clear understanding of who their brand will be exposed to through their participation.

Rather than leaving the meeting with a better understanding of the charity, the business partner leaves the meeting with an awareness of what's in it for them. Unless the charity leader is meeting with the ultimate decision maker, we are relying on those at the meeting to pass on the story of the charity and sharing the passion. Now they can tell the story of why it makes business sense to be involved.

Identifying what's in it for the business partner need not be confined to these meetings. Applications for grants, online submissions and proposal documents usually take a similar approach. The guidelines are normally based on 'tell us what you are going to do and how you will report back'. Sure, there is a need to comply with application or submission criteria, but there is no reason why identifying the benefits for the business can't form part of your submission.

If the author of the grant application or proposal document views it less as a 'donation request' and more as a business submission, the context and content will change. If we seek and treat revenue as donations, the implication is there is very little need to give anything back other than a receipt and a bit of a story. Whether or not they call it such, donors are looking for a return on their donation. If they haven't woken up to the possible returns, it's incumbent on the progressive charity to make that connection.

> Whether or not they call it such, donors are looking for a return on their donation. If they haven't woken up to the possible returns, it's incumbent on the progressive charity to make that connection.

An essential question that should be asked by the charity group heading into each pitch or before the submission of each grant application or proposal should be: 'Is it clear what's in it for them and have I made it easy for them to say yes?'

Leveraging the CSR investment

It is about you.

Australians need to park their humility at the door and accept that a good CSR strategy is an investment. When businesses direct funds or resources away from core business they are depriving someone of a return or entitlement to those resources. Whether it is the partners or directors of the firm, the shareholders, or the employees or their family members who are awarded bonuses at the end of each year, someone is missing out. When funds are directed to a charity or NFP program there should be a return. In chapter 3 we looked at what returns can be expected from an effective CSR strategy, but what about leveraging those returns?

I hope by this stage you have accepted that investment in the CSR space should see a return to business. Even if you won't say it out aloud, please acknowledge it to yourself now, otherwise what I am about to say is irrelevant.

When a business chooses to sponsor an event or support a particular project, the value is not in the sponsorship per se, but in the leverage obtained. The value to a business of committing funds to building a home for children in a developing area of the world is lost if they don't leverage it. And why shouldn't they? It is not wrong to talk about the good that is done, as long as that conversation is in good taste. It is not about being self-congratulatory and taking credit for all that is done; it is an opportunity to acknowledge the difference that has been made.

> The value to a business of committing funds to building a home for children in a developing area of the world is lost if they don't leverage it.

- Invest time at the beginning of the relationship or project to develop a strategy that clearly articulates the terms of the relationship, including the expectations and opportunities, and what measures will be put in place to gauge the change or success that is achieved.

- There is a very real opportunity for progressive charities to lead the discussion with their corporate partners or sponsors about the value that can be realised from a well-planned and well-executed CSR strategy.

- Charities should look to building long-term relationships at the expense of money up front.

- With some 600 000 charities and NFP entities in Australia, it is a crowded marketplace and there is a need to stand out from the rest. Charities need to make it easier for businesses to support them, and to do that they should focus not on how good or needy they are but on what the relationship offers the business partner. Look for an alignment of values and don't be too quick to give away your brand.

- Most charities will be creating experiences for their supporters. Those experiences may be over in a night or a weekend, or may stretch out over a year, but it's safe to assume that it extends beyond what might be the obvious time frame. The business and the charity partner should look to leverage the opportunities to gain maximum value from the investment made.

chapter 9

JOURNEY
to shared value

The current model dictates that the needs of society not met by government or business are left to the charity or for-purpose sector, which does its best to fill the gaps. Most of its funding comes from individuals and the business sector. In his article 'Australian Giving Trends—Recovery Confirmed, Evolution Gains Pace' for JBWere (October 2013), John McLeod notes that 86 per cent of the giving (excluding donations to private ancillary funds) was by individuals.

In addition to demonstrating the importance to charities of individual donors, this finding also highlights the opportunity for business and government to increase their participation in the sector. If the combined contribution to the for-purpose sector by government and business sits at 14 per cent, the obvious question is why is it so low?

Changing the operating model

It might be argued that it is not the responsibility of business to fill the shortfall, that they are already doing their bit by employing those who make the contributions and by paying their taxes along the way. But what if the operating model changed so it was made more attractive to business to engage? What if it was less about *giving* and more about *partnering* that saw returns flow to them through increased revenue, a more engaged workforce and the opening of new markets to do business in?

The current model of donating funds for what can be very little return to the business is limiting. There are of course plenty of areas of return to business from their engagement with the for-purpose sector, including employee engagement, new markets, staff retention, brand enhancement and many others, as covered in chapter 3.

Under the current model the revenue needed to meet social needs can be increased only by the greater generosity of those who give or by expanding the numbers of those who give. As Dan Pallotta notes, giving in the US has remained at around 2 per cent for the past 40 years. The reports of giving in Australia are a little more encouraging, at around 5 per cent. The problem with running campaigns to encourage those who already give to give more or enticing new people into the sector, no matter how successful they might be, is that they too are limiting. This is not to say that we should abandon our efforts to encourage donors. John McLeod's JBWere report shows hopeful trends in the Australian market. The past 15 years have seen a 5 per cent increase in the number of taxpayers claiming a deduction for donations to charity, rising to 38 per cent. The amount that people are donating on a per annum basis has also grown by 6.6 per cent over the past 10 years, outstripping the CPI, which has risen at 2.9 per cent over the same period. Our most generous donors are those of more mature age, with the age group being the first to pass $500 per person in annual contribution.

This growth in giving is certainly promising, but the analysis by JBWere also indicates that it is influenced by the strength of the economy and consumer confidence. Economic uncertainly triggers a drop in both the level of giving and the numbers of people who give. When people become more conservative in their spending because of uncertainty in the market, or when job security is threatened, donations to charities will be influenced negatively. The cost of purchasing the 'feel good' feeling becomes too high and there is less to go around. The knock-on effect of this is that as people lose their jobs, or fear their loss, as a result of a poorly performing economy, demand for the services offered by the for-purpose sector rises.

But as Michael Porter, Professor at Harvard Business School and co-author of *Creating Shared Value*, puts it, 'There is a reason to be optimistic about the future', and that optimism rests in considering how else business can contribute to addressing the problems that society faces other than by creating profits. The old paradigm was that business paid their taxes and employed people, and that was how they contributed to the needs of society. Profit, says Porter, 'was seen as taking away from society, but it is that very profit that enables us to solve the problems of society'. He adds, 'Businesses acting as businesses, not as charitable donors, are the most powerful force for addressing the pressing issues we face. The moment for a new conception of capitalism is now; society's needs are large and growing, while customers, employees, and a new generation of young people are asking business to step up'.

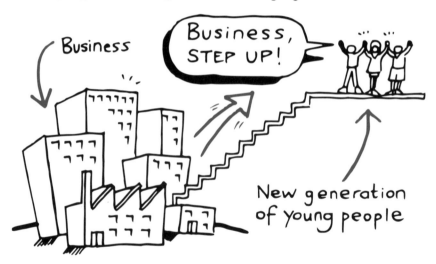

It is the profits that companies are able to generate that offer the scale to take on the challenges in the community that previously have been left to the well-meaning but poorly funded and not always efficient not-for-profit sector. As we have seen, it is access to resources that often defines the scale and scope of their projects.

'Businesses acting as businesses, not as charitable donors, are the most powerful force for addressing the pressing issues we face.'

doing so Mycoskie created both a successful social venture and a very profitable business. While unique companies like TOMS will continue to appear when social entrepreneur meets social need, the bulk of change will come from companies, large and small, as they travel on their values-based journeys. It may be driven by opportunities for new business, to reduce operating costs or to enter new markets, or by the desire to improve their social presence. Whatever the trigger, engaging with the community sector can and should be good for business.

The CSR participation continuum

Most companies with employee numbers reaching into the thousands will have some sort of CSR platform within their organisation. It might be as simple as workplace giving, matching employee contributions or the allocation of time to staff to volunteer once a year with their favourite charity. It would be most unusual for a large company not to have in place some sort of program, no matter how simple. Small to medium-sized companies are more likely to have no formal CSR program in place.

Figure 9.1 (overleaf) shows the various stages on the CSR participation continuum, from entering the space for the first time to assuming a fully integrated shared value model. The journey has three main phases, Prompters, Adopters and Integrators, each of which represents both influential individuals and processes that trigger change.

Doing Good by Doing Good

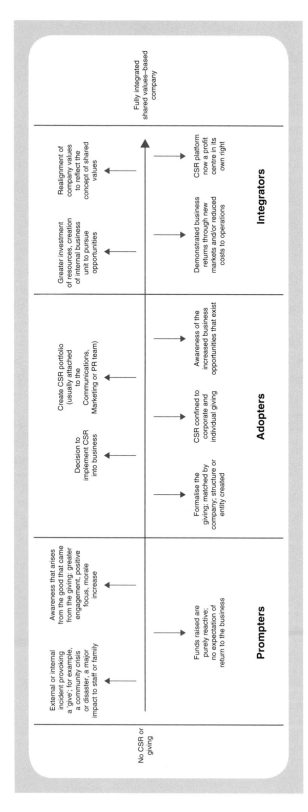

Figure 9.1: the CSR continuum—from entry to fully integrated shared value model

Prompters

These are the events and influential individuals likely to trigger the business to take action. Perhaps an internal or external incident calls for some sort of company response. Often this will be when an employee or a family member experiences a significant crisis or tragedy, such as through illness or accident, and those around them rally together to offer support. Another prompter might be a natural disaster on a local, national or international level.

Often the giving at such times will be based on an emotional response without form or structure, with someone within the company standing up to take the lead, for example in organising fundraising events. The response serves to unite staff across the company behind a shared purpose, bringing together those who previously might not have had reason to interact. With a shared focus, staff will start to engage with their suppliers and/ or consumers on a different level as they encourage them to join in the endeavour, which creates an awareness of the power of engagement. These are the early signs of the returns that a structured CSR program can offer a company, and it's not long before it is recognised that the giving has been good for the business. Unless action is taken at this point, however, the momentum can be lost and the emotion that was driving the initiative passes.

The work done by the Prompters in these initial periods is normally outside their usual commitments. There will be a tolerance from within their business team and their family as they divert their efforts into what all agree is a worthy cause, but if the business is not set up for the sudden reallocation of resources, this tolerance by others in the organisation who must 'pick up the slack' will probably last no longer than the emotion driving the event.

Adopters

Adopters are those within the organisation who take action to see that some structure is brought to the process. They will act either through a desire for the giving to continue, which may be attributable to their proximity to the cause, or because they have identified the benefits to the business.

After the initial flow of giving from employees and the company, there is a realisation that for the giving to continue resources will need to be committed, and the company may consider establishing a legal entity to that end. During these early days the contribution will normally be financial contributions by the employees and/or the company. As the giving continues, the leadership team will look to find a 'home' for this new business project, and it will often become an extension of the work of the marketing, communications or PR team.

For those businesses who adopt a CSR initiative on the back of an external or internal tragedy, over time the initial enthusiasm will naturally cool. The national or international crisis may have dominated the media news, but who keeps the story alive within the business when the TV crews pack up and head on to the next news grab? Who within the business can talk to the change their donation has helped make, or why it is essential that the giving goes on? Perhaps someone else in the company is beset by tragedy—who decides which cause should be supported? How do you say yes to one and no to an equally worthwhile applicant? It is these sorts of challenges that will often persuade the company to shift their focus from a 'cause-related' strategy to a more holistic, values-based position. This is when the company will look to establishing their guiding principles, as outlined in chapter 12. The business has felt the power of engagement, and once experienced this is not something that many will choose to give up.

Integrators

These are the people and processes that are put in place to ensure that the benefits to the business of *doing good by doing good* are realised and embedded. As the maturity of the CSR initiative increases, so too will the allocation of resources. Separate business units will be established to identify new opportunities, undertake research and outline the scope of those opportunities. Increased funding will be allocated to those initiatives that bring measurable returns on the investment over the longer term.

The journey along the continuum towards shared value will see the business incorporate new values to reflect the importance of the new position. Those companies furthest along the continuum towards a true social venture entity will see their work addressing society's challenges in a profitable way as one, if not *the*, reason for their very existence. Are they making a profit in order to tackle some of the community's biggest challenges, or are they incidentally providing an answer to these questions while running a for-profit company? The distinction is blurred in the fully integrated shared value model.

> With the right measures, alignment to the values of the business and vertical support through the org chart, there is no reason why all businesses shouldn't be *doing good by doing good*.

We must accept, of course, that many companies either have no desire to pursue this path or are committed to taking much smaller steps while ensuring they maximise the return on their give. The shared value model as exemplified by Unilever Global or TOMS doesn't have to be embraced for smaller companies to see their CSR strategy becoming a profit centre in its own right. With the right measures, alignment to the values of the business and vertical support through the org chart, there is no reason why all businesses shouldn't be *doing good by doing good*.

Shared value and innovation

We can call it shared value, blended value, conscious capitalism or a combination thereof. The name is less important than the opportunities that changing the CSR mindset from one of corporate philanthropy to one of engagement for mutual benefit can deliver. When companies embrace the opportunity to tackle social problems that have gone unanswered or have been subject to no more than bandaid solutions, innovation can lead the way.

The corporate giant GE has coined the term *ecomagination*: 'GE's business strategy to create new value for customers, investors and society by helping to solve energy, efficiency and water challenges. It is our belief that, through a constant commitment to innovation, we can design and deliver great economics as well as great environmental performance'.

Ecomagination, as characterised by GE, sits nicely within the definition of shared value. The concept as put forward by Porter and Kramer includes the broader supply chain and the building of local clusters, but the end result is the same—business deriving a commercial benefit from meeting society's needs.

The returns that GE attributes to its ecomagination business strategy are staggering and a testament to the value of bringing innovation to these opportunities:

R&D

Ecomagination commenced in 2005 and since that time GE has invested $12 billion in research and development. For the five-year period from 2010 to 2015 its commitment to R&D is $10 billion in the development of technology that benefits both its customers and the environment.

Products

Since the launch of ecomagination more than $160 billion has been realised in revenues. For the period of 2010–15, ecomagination is set to be a larger part of GE's sales with the company committing to growing ecomagination revenues at double the rate of its total company revenue.

Energy/GHG

Since 2004 GE has reduced its greenhouse gas emissions by 32 per cent against the 2004 baseline. In 2010 GE reported an 18 per cent reduction in its energy consumption from the 2004 baseline which it attributes in part to its focus on improved energy efficiencies that have been implemented in the company.

Water

The amount of freshwater used by GE in its operations has reduced by 45 per cent against the 2006 baseline. The savings in energy and water alone have realised a $300 million cost reduction.

Keep public informed

GE has a commitment towards communication and transparency. The production of its annual 'Global Impact Report' and consultation with stakeholders across borders, allows it to spotlight and develop the best ideas on the creation and use of power.

GE's experience is that each dollar it invests in R&D in line with its ecomagination business strategy will produce $10 in new revenue. Figure 9.2 (overleaf) illustrates some common returns.

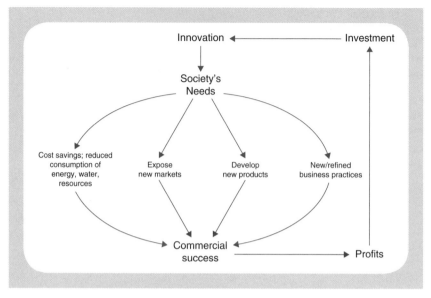

Figure 9.2: the path from innovation to commercial success to reinvestment in innovation for tackling social needs

A focus on integrating CSR or shared value across the entire business when leading with innovation can reasonably prompt:

- reduced consumption and spend on resources such as power, water and waste

- the emergence of new markets that under previous models were seen as unprofitable

- the development of new products that might be at a lower cost entry point

- a change in operations or business practices that brings greater efficiencies.

In addition to their role as innovators, companies embracing the concept of shared value are redefining who they are. Nestlé is a leader in this area for the work it has done in repositioning itself with regard to the supply chain and building clusters for manufacturing. Michael Porter sees the change from its traditional positioning as a 'food and beverage company' to a 'nutrition, health and wellness company' as reflecting a change in how it views itself, the products it is offering and the way its customers see it.

Companies embracing shared value are, as part of that process, questioning what they do and what they stand for. The definition then starts to reflect the community needs they are meeting, as opposed to the products they are producing. Nestlé is addressing some of society's biggest challenges around health care by changing its offerings and changing what it is about.

> Companies embracing shared value are, as part of that process, questioning what they do and what they stand for.

The critics of shared value

> The opportunity to create economic value through creating societal value will be one of the most powerful forces driving growth in the global economy.
>
> —Michael Porter

The critics of the concept of shared value suggest, among other things, that the concept offers nothing new. Is there a huge difference between *conscious capitalism*, as already discussed, and the concept of *blended value*, as developed in the work of Jed Emerson? Do these simply offer an expanded view of CSR beyond corporate philanthropy?

Critics of Porter and Kramer's *Creating Shared Value* argue that their view of CSR is too narrow and doesn't reflect the broad approach that can be adopted, and that adopting this narrow view widens the gap between CSR and shared value. The criticism is not of the principles or concepts behind shared value, but of Porter and Kramer's grand claims about the radical shift it offers to the business world and the future of capitalism. This becomes a debate over semantics. If we agree there are benefits for the business community and society at large, then I suggest we embrace those parts that resonate and reject those that don't.

- Various names and terms have been coined around the concept of shared value, but all are about bringing business closer to the community sector so they work in partnership to address social needs, offering benefits to all involved.

- The concept of shared value advances the traditional models of CSR and corporate philanthropy. Reaching the true potential offered by shared value will often require an investment in innovation that leads to productivity gains, new markets, refined operating procedures, new products and a reduction in the spend on resources.

- Embarking on the journey towards shared value requires considerable cultural change. The senior leadership team needs to be not only on board but championing the change process.

- Companies that seek full integration of a shared value model often realign their values towards their sustainability position.

chapter 10

MEASURING
and reporting

There are numerous entry points into the world of giving. Many businesses will start with cash donations, perhaps supporting their staff with an annual day off to volunteer. Not unlike most investments, the more time you devote to understanding the area, the more intelligent and mature your investment becomes. As the significance of the investment grows so does the desire to measure and report on that investment.

There are many options when it comes to measuring and reporting in this area. The simplest form of measurement is aligned to the simplest form of giving. If your engagement is limited to the donation of a sum of money, then the reporting too is that simple. At the end of the financial year the company carves off $50 000, which it gives to one or many charities or causes. The reporting will amount to a line on the balance sheet that records that transaction. There may be an article in the internal newsletter or a feature story on the intranet, but often that is the sum total of the reporting.

When the engagement becomes more mature, so too does the giving. Nick Dowling, CEO of the Jellis Craig Group, comments, 'As a commercial business it would be easier from a time perspective just to channel off a portion of the share of profits that we make every year and feel good about it'. This had indeed been the previous model of CSR strategy adopted by Jellis Craig, when the give was measured by the cash it had raised and donated to its charity partners. There was no acknowledgement of the dedication of resources in the management of its position. Nick knew that when the company took on fundraising activities, the bulk of the load was carried by head office staff.

But Jellis Craig made the decision that simply channeling off a share of the profit was not going to bring the level of engagement they were looking for. In the development of their strategy they looked beyond the donation of funds to a commitment that included:

- formation of a legal entity within the group
- establishment of a foundation committee

- commitment to various community-based activities, such as:
  - Field of Women BCNA
  - Run Melbourne
  - Hands Across the Water bike ride
  - Red Cross blood donations.

The resources it commits to its program of giving quickly heads towards matching the level of cash it is providing. So how should this be reflected in the annual report it prepares for its stakeholders at the end of year? Should it simply record the amount of money it donates or should the allocation of resources towards ensuring the programs are a success be included as well?

Optus's contribution to the community in pure dollar terms through community support initiatives such as direct cash funding, in-kind support, leverage, customer initiatives, staff time and workplace giving was reported in its 2014 sustainability report as $9.7 million, with direct grants reported as just $300 000.

Is Optus right in including all of the costs, in-kind support and staff time it allocates to ensuring the program is a success? Of course it is. Failure to identify the true costs of the program not only would be wrong on an accounting basis but would make the accurate measurement of success or failure impossible. Whatever the business, when determining the true cost of doing business you don't *not* include the non-sales areas that don't generate a profit. It only makes sense to identify and report accurately the true cost of your CSR platform, not just the dollar contribution that reaches your partners.

> Failure to identify the true costs of the program not only would be wrong on an accounting basis but would make the accurate measurement of success or failure impossible.

When I talk with prospective clients about their CSR strategy I tell them, 'If your CSR strategy is not a profit centre for your business, it is not as effective as it can be'. To determine whether or not the strategy is a profit centre, we have to know the true cost of executing the strategy.

The past 20 years has seen the emergence of groups who have set about measuring and reporting on the effectiveness of CSR programs by business. At the same time there is an increasing awareness of the effectiveness of programs beyond giving cash and how they are good for business.

Benchmarking and measuring

In 1994 LBG (formerly London Benchmarking Group) developed a model for measuring and reporting the value of community investment by businesses. This model is now used by more than 300 companies around the world. It has around 50 members in Australia and New Zealand, including Optus, NAB, Myer, Medibank and many others.

The LBG chapter in the Australia–New Zealand region is supported by a small administrative team. The lifeblood of the chapter is the Steering Committee, which is made up of members from industry who are committed to growing the model of measuring and reporting their community investment.

Models and reporting from organisations such as LBG become a richer and more factual representation of the *entire* community investment as their membership base grows. The Steering Committee is very aware of this, which is why growing the membership base falls within its ambit. Currently the membership is diverse as it is large, with less traditional and certainly smaller organisations, whose strategies around community investment are less mature, enter the group. Businesses just entering the space of community investment, or whose involvement is limited to financial donations, may not at first see the value in measuring and reporting their investment, or will see their investment simply in terms of the sum total of the dollars they give away.

LBG utilises a framework for measuring the inputs, outputs and the impact made as a result of an organisation's contribution (see figure 10.1, overleaf).

LBG effectively measures *inputs*—whatever has been contributed, including cash, time, in-kind support and, importantly, the management costs of maintaining a CSR program. Members of the LBG community have an average of 4.5 full time employees working within their various community engagement programs. This figure relates mainly to the larger corporate entities with the capacity to allocate a head count to their CSR initiatives.

Outputs refers to what is delivered in terms of how many are reached, how many are involved and what types of activities are run. An organisation would report on the hard evidence of the program. It is not about the success or change that resulted, but about how many were affected in a measurable way.

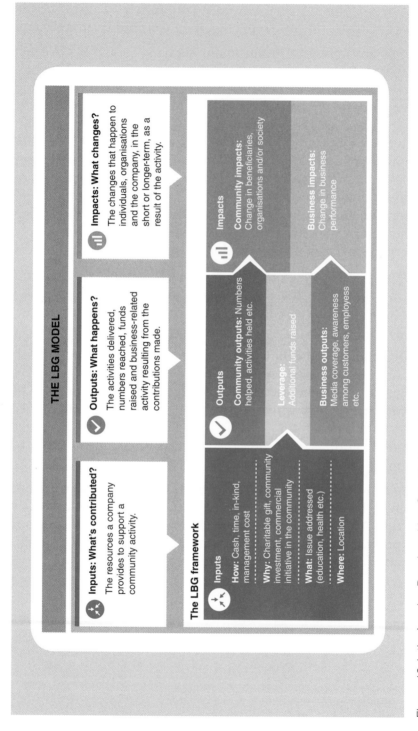

Figure 10.1: the London Benchmarking Group's measuring model
Reproduced with permission from LBG Australia & New Zealand (http://www.lbg-australia.com)

Impacts seeks to measure the changes achieved as a result of the program—what difference was made, not just on the receiver but importantly on the business itself. Has the program produced measurable employee development opportunities? Has there been a change in customer loyalty as a result of the program? Can new clients or customers be attributed to the program? It is often too easy to focus on the measurement of the success for the end user and miss the opportunity to measure the success of the program internally. Conversely, has the program consumed more resources than anticipated with more limited benefits to the end user, so that the program is not deemed to be worth duplicating in its current format? These types of judgements can be made only when all of the information is measured and reported.

> It is often too easy to focus on the measurement of the success for the end user and miss the opportunity to measure the success of the program internally.

A priority for LBG has been to assist its membership move from a focus on what is contributed in the form of inputs to really consider their outputs and, most importantly, the impact their programs are having. Navigating this is a challenge as the impact is so much more difficult to measure than something solid such as 'we contributed $250 000 last year', but when an understanding is gained of the impact, the gap between philanthropy and shared value is increasingly diminished.

The Optus student2student program offers a good illustration of the LBG model of measuring inputs, outputs and impacts (see illustration overleaf).

The resources that Optus committed to the student2student program included the gift to each student of a handset. As the program expanded from the initial pilot of 50 student pairs, Optus staff and family members were invited into the program as reading mentors. Also included were the administrative resources from Optus to develop, research and execute the program. In addition it provided training to each student in the responsible use of a mobile phone.

The outputs are measured in the numbers of students who have passed through the 18-week program, with 525 reading pairs participating nationally. An accurate total would far exceed this when including those who have been made aware of the program through family, teachers and other students both as mentors and mentees.

Ninety-three per cent of students improved their reading age and 96 per cent of parents noted improvements in their child's reading. That is a clear, measurable outcome. Added to that was the experience shared by the staff and their families, which on anecdotal evidence was enriching for all involved. Through the education programs it attached to the rollout of the handsets, Optus was able to provide new mobile phone owners with important practical tips on how to effectively manage the credit attached to these phones. For the disadvantaged communities in which it was working, the importance of these lessons should not be underestimated.

The student2student program could readily be measured in terms of the input of resources such as hardware and time against the outputs and impacts of numbers involved and improvement to literacy standards. But is that a true measure of the reach of the program? For example, how many of the following may have been areas of real impact?

- What was the change in view of the children of Optus staff involved in the program on how a corporate interacts with the community?

- How many of these children have had a chance to participate with their parents in 'giving' in a currency other than money?

- Do Optus staff who have been involved in the program feel greater loyalty to their employer for creating an experience they could share with their children?

- Do the staff have an increased sense of pride in the company they work for?

- How many of their children have an increased loyalty to the brand as a result of their exposure?

- How many of the children from disadvantaged communities were introduced to a brand and have become new customers?

- Was there any positive press coverage of the program?

- Was there any improvement in business-to-business relationships on the back of this program?

- It was reported that 93 per cent of students enjoyed improvements to their reading age but what of the impact of that improvement on their schooling, subsequent employment opportunities and even diversion rates from the criminal justice system?

The Optus student2student case study illustrates the kinds of areas that may or may not be recorded, and the difficulty in trying to measure the total impact of a CSR program. If

Measuring and reporting

measurement of the impact is based on knowns and unknowns, what of the way resources or contributions are made?

One of the most effective pieces of analysis LBG provides is a breakdown of how its members contribute. It has been collecting data since 2006 and eight years of reporting has revealed marked consistencies in contribution.

As shown in figure 10.2, it measures contribution in four areas:

- cash
- time
- in-kind
- management costs.

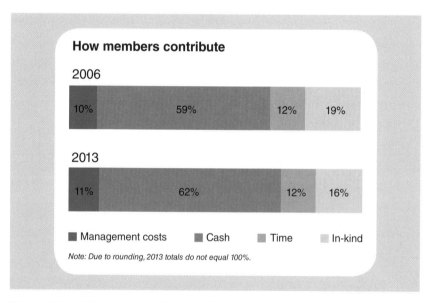

Figure 10.2: LBG analysis of CSR contribution — comparison over time

What the figures demonstrate is that over an eight-year reporting period the distribution over the four areas of measurement remains remarkably consistent. The cash contributions over eight years averages out at 60.25 per cent, while the management costs over the same period average 10.1 per cent.

Two conclusions can be drawn from these figures: first, the management costs in running the CSR programs are significant and need to be accounted for in the corporate contribution; secondly, the cash contribution is very high, and I would predict that over the next five years that figure will fall if those companies participating in the benchmarking remain the same.

This conclusion reflects the shift by those companies who have been involved in this space for some time towards a model of greater shared value. As they progress along the continuum towards fully integrated shared value, their contribution will be aligned less to the cash donated and more to the in-kind support. For example, in the guest-led mentoring program set up by the Sheraton Grande Sukhumvit (as described in the case study in chapter 2), the cash contribution by the hotel to its CSR program is zero, but its leverage and in-kind support is huge.

Optus offers another example: its cash contribution is a mere 3.2 per cent of its total give. As a company develops its maturity in this space the trend is away from direct cash donations and towards a recognition that a greater difference can occur through the leverage brought to the table. More and more, CEOs like Nick Dowling from Jellis Craig appreciate that the true value to the company and indeed to its charity partners is not in the cash given away but in the experiences shared.

Where the change in reporting may not indicate the decrease I predict is among new members of the LBG community who are just entering the CSR space and whose contribution is heavily weighted towards cash donations— because that's what so many do at the start of their journey.

> The true value to the company and indeed to its charity partners is not in the cash given away but in the experiences shared.

Reporting indices

LBG is but one of several reporting indices that allow the measurement, reporting and benchmarking of companies who are involved in CSR beyond corporate philanthropy. Here are some of the other indices that are widely used for benchmarking.

Global Reporting Initiative (GRI)

GRI is an international not-for-profit (its secretariat is based in the Netherlands) with over 600 members worldwide. Founded in the US in 1997 with the core purpose of serving as an environmental reporting agency, its reporting framework has expanded to become more inclusive, providing measures of social, economic and governance issues. The latest framework, G4, was released in 2013.

GRI defines a sustainability report as 'a report published by a company or organization about the economic, environmental and social impacts caused by its everyday activities'. The framework enables its members to report on the four key areas of sustainability—economic, environmental, social and governance.

GRI is represented in Australia by the GRI Focal Point, which is hosted by the St James Ethics Centre.

More information on GRI is available via its website: www. globalreporting.org.

Corporate Responsibility Index (CR Index)

The CR index, another benchmarking group out of the UK, was formed in 2002. It also has a presence in Australia. Its aim is to help member companies to:

- *Identify*—gaps for improvement and reinforce good practice
- *Track*—progress over time and drive continuous improvement
- *Benchmark*—against peers and leading practice
- *Engage*—board members and raise awareness internally.

The tools it offers allow companies to measure themselves and report both publicly or privately. The public disclosure allows companies to be included in the annual CR Index ranking, while private participation suits companies who are 'not ready to disclose their performance'. Companies participating in the CR Index include Unilever, Heineken, and Marks & Spencer.

More information on the CR Index is available via its website: www.bitc.org.uk.

Dow Jones Sustainability Indices (DJSI)

The DJSI, launched in 1999, claims to be the first global sustainability benchmark. It tracks the stock performance of 'the world's leading companies in terms of economic, environmental and social criteria ... they serve as benchmarks for investors who integrate sustainability considerations into their portfolios, and provide an effective engagement platform for companies who want to adopt sustainable best practices'.

More information on the DJSI is available via its website: www.sustainability-indices.com.

Measuring and reporting

ISO 26000 Social Responsibility

In addition to benchmarking opportunities the International Organisation for Standardization has an ISO for social responsibility, ISO 26000, more commonly known as ISO SR. Unlike many of the ISO standards used to measure or demonstrate compliance and/or certification, ISO SR is 'intended to provide organisations with guidance concerning social responsibility and can be used as part of public policy activities'. Launched in November 2010, it aims to provide practical guidelines to implement social responsibility, identify and engage stakeholders, and to enhance the credibility of reports and claims made about social responsibility.

While the standard does not allow a user to attach certification, which is the norm with ISO standards, it does allow for self-declaration based on self-assessment and evaluation against the framework of ISO SR. The use of the ISO framework in conjunction with some of the other reporting indices enriches the results and benchmarking capabilities.

ISO SR states that the social responsibility of an organisation is to ensure that its decisions contribute to sustainable development, health and community welfare; consider stakeholder expectations; comply with the law and behavioural norms; and are integrated throughout the organisation.

Organisations using the ISO should follow these principles:

- accountability for the organisation's impact on society and the environment
- transparency in all decisions and activities that impact on society and the environment
- ethical behaviour at all times
- respect for the organisation's employees
- acceptance of the law
- respect for international norms of behaviour and for human rights.

Following on from the key principles are the seven core subjects that organisations should focus on:

- organisational governance
- human rights
- labour practices
- environment
- fair operating practices
- consumer issues
- community involvement and development.

The question has to be asked, who benefits from taking your CSR reporting to this level? Will small to medium-sized organisations benefit by implementing these principles, and at what cost? A common view of this type of accreditation is that it is often better to not have it than to not to meet the accreditation standards, or worse still to have met them at one point but to have areas of non-compliance.

So who benefits from standards such as ISO SR? Those most likely to benefit are corporates who are working across international borders and want to demonstrate that their supply chain meets international standards around the labour practices and human rights.

The real effectiveness of the ISO standards and their level of applicability will take time to emerge. Introduced in 2010, it is too early to draw and conclusions on their success, but with the passage of time the demand by those entering into international trade will be the true measure.

How and what to report

A plethora of styles can be adopted in communicating with the key stakeholders on the activities undertaken in the year of reporting. Many of the larger corporates produce their sustainability reports in line with their annual reporting on business, some of which combine both. A lot of these reports focus on inputs and outputs, with fewer focusing on impact. Of those reporting the impact, even fewer take the next step to report on the management costs associated with their programs.

Many of the reports will focus on the cash given, the water saved and the hours devoted by employees. They can be a bit of a chest-thumping exercise and tend to be somewhat vanilla in their offerings. The most engaging reports are those that tell the stories of how it has impacted on the lives of those in the community who have benefited. For most readers, a reduction in greenhouse emissions or the fact that 5392 employees were involved in a day of volunteering doesn't bring a lot of excitement. How about reporting on the experience of two of the volunteers—how they spent their day and the names of those they helped? Statistics and figures aren't all that exciting unless you are an actuary; stories are what people want to hear.

> The most engaging reports are those that tell the stories of how it has impacted on the lives of those in the community who have benefited.

The stakeholders who are likely to be interested readers will include:

- customers
- employees
- consumers
- investors
- business partners
- government agencies
- non-profit organisations
- the general community.

Each will probably have a different bias towards the information they are seeking, which will fall under a number of broader themes:

People

- workplace diversity
- targeted employment practices
- employee resource assistance
- focus on health and welfare

Giving — corporate/employee

- total cash given by way of direct funding
- employee contributions in time and money
- employee volunteer hours, matched or otherwise
- in-kind support
- leverage

Environmental

- reduction in use of water and non-renewable energy
- landfill avoidance
- reduction in greenhouse gas emissions

- investment in environmentally sustainable buildings and manufacturing
- logistics and fleet

Supply chain

- sourced from sustainable operations
- compliant with human rights standards
- compliant with accepted labour practices.

Voluntary reporting

Unlike financial reporting for companies, which is mandatory at the end of the financial year, reporting on activities around CSR programs remains voluntary. Those that do report on the environmental and social activities do so without set reporting criteria and can choose what they include and what they don't.

There are a number of obstacles to full and frank reporting by business. Simon Robinson, a director with LBG in Australia– New Zealand, notes the following impediments to the type of reporting that might otherwise be possible:

- Many businesses still view their CSR work as *charity* so don't apply the same rigour as they do to other areas of their business.

- There is a lack of executive leadership across corporate Australia promoting the necessity of reporting and the value of community investment to business and communities.

- In part because of this lack of leadership at the most senior levels, business generally doesn't commit the resources required.

- Business struggles to measure the *impact* its programs are having.

- Existing methodologies to assess impacts can often be too complex and too expensive.

Research conducted by the Centre for Corporate Public on behalf of LBG Australia found that one of the main obstacles to impact assessment is a lack of clear intent behind why companies start their community investment work and what they hope to gain from it. Very few companies are measuring and reporting on their impact.

Without clear guidelines or reporting criteria, corporates can set their own measures and report as they choose. This raises the risk that the data relating to community in sustainability reports they issue at the end of their reporting cycle become more of a PR document, which may throw into question the authenticity of their entire program.

The number of benchmarking groups and measuring indices like LBG is growing. Progress in this area is being impeded not so much by a lack of agencies that are there to measure and report, but by a lack of desire by business to engage in meaningful and measured reporting.

Compulsory reporting

The state of California, in the US, may very well be the first legislature to bring into law compulsory reporting connected to CSR. On 1 January 2012 the *California Transparency in Supply Chains Act 2010* (also known as Senate Bill 657 or SB 657) was enacted.

The legislation that was enacted in 2012 applies to retailers and manufacturers who have gross annual receipts that exceed $100 million. The purpose of the legislation is to require retailers and manufacturers to disclose their efforts to eradicate slavery and human trafficking from their supply chain. A condition of the act is that the retailers and manufacturers who fit within the requirement of the legislation provide their customers with information concerning their supply chain and those who contribute to the manufacture of the goods. Effectively, the legislation is forcing the retailers and manufacturers to disclose to the end customer where the goods they are buying are made, where the materials are sourced and who has contributed to the manufacturing process. It is giving the customers the information that they may seek to make informed purchasing decisions.

One outcome of SB 657 has been the resource KnowTheChain, whose purpose is, with a number of partner organisations, to analyse and measure the companies within California who are affected by the legislation and to report on their compliance. It has evaluated 500 retail or manufacturing corporations on whom the legislation impacts and holds the reports of those companies on its website. It doesn't advocate for those who are reporting and complying with the requirements of SB 657, nor does it call on the public to boycott those who have not complied. It simply brings the information together in one place to promote discussion and awareness.

Compulsory reporting in accordance with SB 657 is a huge step towards putting the information in the public domain and allowing informed decisions by customers. Some of the companies reported on the KnowTheChain website as not complying make broad, sweeping statements about how they support equality and the good for all. You can almost see the company spokesman reading this statement, a cape across his shoulders, gazing heroically into the distance.

In its statement posted on the KnowTheChain website, Apple was more specific when outlining its activity. For example, 'In addition to regularly scheduled audits, we conduct a number of surprise audits during which our team visits a supplier unannounced and insists on inspecting the facility within an hour of arrival. We conducted 28 of these surprise audits in 2012. During our regular audits, we may also ask a supplier to immediately show us portions of a facility that are not scheduled for review.'

Lodging such a statement doesn't mean Apple doesn't have a case to answer or that mention of these audits should necessarily persuade us that it is in compliance across the globe, but it does give evidence of the work it is doing.

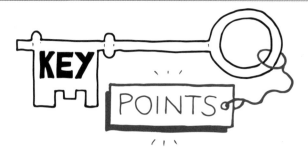

The key takeaways from this chapter include the following:

- Reporting on commitment to the community should include not only the cash donated, but the in-kind support, volunteering and, importantly, the administration costs of the program—how much does it cost you to run your CSR platform?

- Measurement should include the cost of the inputs, what the outputs are and what impacts are made by the programs. There will be some easily identifiable outputs and impacts, but the true value of the program may be hidden. Search for the bigger picture.

- Benchmarking allows you to compare your activities across your industry and with other industries. The more participants that report and measure their activities, the richer the pool to benchmark against.

- The cash amount given to partners will fall on a percentage basis of the total give as your giving and manner of participation mature and change.

- Tell the stories of the difference that has been made. There is often a reluctance, particularly among smaller and medium-sized businesses, to spend much time talking about their programs or the changes they bring. But without advocacy, fewer people inside the business will be inspired to participate. Storytelling, with humility, will inspire other businesses who are not yet engaged to participate in a CSR program.

Measuring and reporting

chapter 11

VALUE OF
shared experiences

In chapter 2 we looked at the various ways in which both corporates and individuals can engage in the for-purpose space. We considered the worth of building a strategic plan around this investment and the value of creating an experience as opposed to making a cash donation.

In this chapter I'll spend more time considering the value of engineering shared experiences. I want to look at the value of these experiences from the perspective of the community group with reference to the work of three particular charities. I firmly believe that if a charity gets the experience right, they need have no worries about sourcing the next dollar. The value for the business partner is that the very experience in which they are participating to create value for their charity partner may be the best engagement tool they ever use.

The model illustrated in figure 11.1 is not confined to building successful partnerships between business and charity. It may equally be applied to our personal relationships or to building stronger teams. If we engineer shared experiences, which is a fundamental role of business leaders, partners and parents, we are likely to build more successful relationships. Who has teenage boys who spend more time interacting on Xbox Live with other players they are likely never to meet, or teenage girls who spend more time on Facebook, Snapchat or whatever the next social network might be, than sitting around the dinner table having meaningful conversations with their own family? What modern family today wouldn't benefit from more shared experiences?

> If we engineer shared experiences, which is a fundamental role of business leaders, partners and parents, we are likely to build more successful relationships.

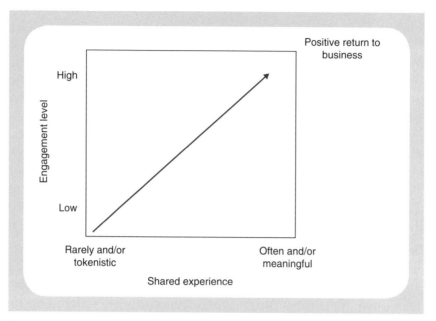

Figure 11.1: increased engagement = increased returns to your business

If we want to build stronger teams within our organisations, we must get out of the conference room and engineer shared experiences. Too much time and money is spent on the logic behind engagement. The richer and the more meaningful those experiences are, the more likely they are to bring results. Whether it be successful sporting teams or groups who have faced extreme adversity, it is the shared experience that unites them. In my earlier career as a forensic investigator I learned much about crisis situations. The experiences I shared in this challenging work created bonds between team members that, unless you were part of them, you could not understand.

The three charities profiled here—Hands Across the Water, OzHarvest and the Humpty Dumpty Foundation—operate in very different areas and support very different communities, but each relies on shared experiences as part of its success. Naturally the first of them is the one that is closest to my heart.

Hands Across the Water

I established Hands Across the Water after working as a forensic investigator in Thailand following the 2004 Boxing Day tsunami, where I led national and international forensic teams in the identification of the thousands of poor souls who lost their lives in the tragedy. During my time in Thailand I was introduced to a number of children who had lost their homes, their parents and, in many cases, their extended family too. When I met the children they were all living in a tent, but not as some temporary stopgap—it was their home. After meeting these kids I made a commitment to do something to change their environment as best I could.

In the beginning I did what most charities do. You use whatever means you have to raise money. You have a goal, you talk about that and ask people to buy into your dream and give you money. That's usually pretty much where the value exchange begins and ends. I was fortunate that in the early days I had a unique platform from which to promote the charity, albeit in a very soft-sell kind of way. After leading the Australian and international teams in Thailand, and having performed a similar role in Bali after the bombings, I was invited onto the corporate speaking circuit to share my stories on leadership, among other topics. I would go on to work for Interpol in the counterterrorism space, spend time with the United Nations Office on Drugs and Crime, and also deploy into Saudi Arabia and Japan when disasters hit those countries.

These experiences led me on a journey around the world, sharing the lessons learned from working in these areas and building teams. Each time I spoke at a conference I would also share the stories of building Hands and the challenges in doing so. The more I spoke, the bigger Hands became; and the bigger Hands became, the more I spoke. The knock-on effect was that Hands was able to start assisting many more children than those that first came to us following the tsunami. We would go on to operate across the breadth of Thailand in seven remote locations, caring for children who had lost their parents, children with HIV and girls rescued from the sex trafficking industry.

But as Hands grew—and it grew quite quickly—I began to reflect on our success in growing at the rate we were in such a competitive space. What became clear to me was the value we were offering our supporters. It wasn't the timeliness of our communication or the glossy thank-you packages after a donation; it happened on a more meaningful and personal level for them.

What we had stumbled across was the power of creating shared experiences, the concept I now know as *creating shared value*, which Simon Sinek identifies as meeting a personal need within the supporter.

Sinek talks about *why* people and companies are successful, and the importance of getting clear on that. He looks at what it was that drove 250 000 people to come together in one place, Washington DC, in 1963, to hear one man speak. The man, Dr Martin Luther King Jr., brought people together without an invitation, without a group text message or a Facebook invite. Sinek challenges the thought that they came together to hear Dr King speak; he suggests they came because to do so met a need within themselves. They came because of what it was giving them as individuals and the need it was meeting.

And this is what Hands stumbled across several years ago; it's why we are successful and why I believe we are about 'providing meaningful experiences'. We are creating opportunities for our supporters to share experiences and along their journey to meet a need deep inside themselves. Some will acknowledge this, some won't, and some won't even realise that's what's occurring. It took me almost eight years of running Hands to realise what we are really about. Sure, we are bringing change to the lives of children. I know that, but for our efforts, many of the children in our HIV home would not be alive today. They had been dying every month, sometimes every week. After we took up responsibility for those children, there were no more deaths. Many of them were cured of AIDS; they still have HIV of course, but they no longer have AIDS.

The shared experiences that we have engineered here at Hands are best illustrated by the bike rides that we lead in Thailand. It's important to know the story behind them to appreciate where we sit today and the real value in creating experiences to build engagement.

In late 2008 the idea of riding from Bangkok to Khao Lak, a distance of 800 kilometres, over eight days, was floated past me almost as a throwaway line. But I was tempted, and soon there were two of us, each committed to raising $10000 in sponsorship. At the time neither of us was a bike rider or even owned a bike. We left in January 2009 with 17 riders, and the Hands rides were underway.

Returning after that first ride with aches and pains from which I felt I might never recover, it took a little time before I began wrestling with the idea of repeating the experience. In 2010 we headed off for a second time with 34 riders, a number of whom were returning for the second time.

By then the interest in the following year's ride was such that I felt we needed to create two rides rather than keep expanding the numbers, so we didn't detract from the nature of the shared experience. In January 2011 we would leave Bangkok and ride with one group covering the 800 km course. Two days after completion I returned to Bangkok and joined the second group to ride another 800 kilometres.

The momentum continued to increase and in 2012 we changed it up a little. We started the first ride in early January, riding from Nong Khai in the far north-east of Thailand, down the Mekong River for eight days before finishing at our HIV centre,

Home Hug, in Yasothon. Two days later we picked up another group and rode from Bangkok to Khao Lak.

In 2012 we had 59 riders across both rides, each raising $10 000 as well as paying for all their own expenses. After the 2012 ride we saw huge growth in participants, money raised and, very interestingly, a number of return riders. In 2013 on our northern ride 79 per cent of riders had ridden with us at least once before; some were back for their second or third ride, and some had never missed a year riding with us.

When we opened the registration list in 2012 for the 2013 ride, the places sold out in three weeks. We had never before sold out a ride and here we had done it in just three weeks. I wondered if we would match this extraordinary success when we opened registration for the 2014 rides on 1 March 2013. We not only matched it — we sold out in three days!

We were now raising well over three-quarters of a million dollars from our bike rides and were selling out in a matter of days. But something interesting started to happen. Instead of people asking for a spot on the ride for themselves or their colleagues, organisations were asking for an entire ride for themselves. They were looking for us to add new rides to our calendar, but they wanted them to be 'closed' rides just for themselves.

Our first closed ride was in 2013 with Family Business Australia, a national body supporting family business and the owners of those businesses. In February 2014 we held our second closed ride for a group of small-business owners and entrepreneurs, who had 30 riders on a cut-down version of the ride over five days, covering 500 kilometres, each raising $5000.

The riding calendar of 2014–15 is set to be our busiest yet with seven rides, five of which will be closed or private rides. We will see over 275 riders partake in one of our bike rides and we expect to raise over $2.5 million in the six-month period we have people on the road.

So is the rate of selling out the rides continuing to rise or have we topped out? On 1 March 2014, when the 2015 rides were opened, we sold out two rides in 90 minutes, and by the close of the first day we had 136 riders (from a maximum of 150) who would ride with us across three rides. Each of these riders is committed to raising a minimum $10 000 and paying for all their own expenses; 26 of the riders have committed to riding 1600 kilometres, meaning they have to raise $20 000 and take close to a month off work for the privilege of doing so. Equally staggering, 52 per cent of the riders in January alone are return riders.

In the space of five years we went from 17 riders, five of whom were members of my own family, and raising $173 000, to 250 riders raising $2.5 million. How to explain such phenomenal growth?

It's because of the shared experience. It comes back to what Simon Sinek says: each of the riders is doing it for themselves. That may be a little contentious and it may even offend some first-time riders who believe they are only doing it for the kids in Thailand.

A number of things make the experience so engaging. It's not just the achievement of raising $10 000. It's not the accomplishment of safely navigating your bike 800 kilometres through the heat and challenges on the road, and it's not just arriving at the home of the children who we have been raising money for. It's the totality of the experience and sharing something so amazing with others. Some of their fellow riders they will know already, some they will not, but often the riders return home with lifelong friends. That's the value of a shared experience.

So what are the five keys to the success of the rides and indeed of Hands itself?

- We provide a meaningful experience for supporters looking to engage on a level beyond simply donating a sum of money. Every supporter who participates in a ride will have engaged on average 100 people whose level of interaction will be limited to the donation of money. Our growth can be attributed in part to the experience of each rider, which then becomes their story, and many of those 100 people who previously only donated money are converted from passive donors to active supporters.

- The meaningful experience is one that is shared with others of a similar mindset. Seth Godin, in his book *Tribes*, articulates the human characteristic of wanting to be part of a group that shares a connection, passion and often a common leader: a tribe. Godin believes that tribes are behind every successful brand, organisation, politician, non-profit and cause. And yet, he laments, it can seem almost impossible to attract a tribe. The tribe we at Hands build is one that legitimises the desire of all grown adults to dress in Lycra and hang out with others of like mind, or have I got that confused with my personal desire?

- We provide an opportunity for people to step into an arena that is foreign to them. We have supporters who are already avid riders before coming to Hands, but the level of fundraising we require is new. Similarly, we have people who have supported charity before but have never considered riding 800 kilometres. One or other aspect of the ride is likely to be new to them—unless of course they are return riders.

- We are able to welcome the riders or supporters into the homes and lives of those whom they have supported, and this is a powerful experience. To see the difference they have made, the tangible results of their efforts, satisfies the 'but for' test.

- On a deeper level, Hands offers those who choose to support our work a high degree of confidence in what we are doing and where their money is going.

Value of shared experiences

OzHarvest

Another charity offering meaningful experiences is Sydney-based OzHarvest, founded by the lovely Ronni Kahn to capitalise on an opportunity where the need was easy to identify. With a professional background in events management, running events of all sizes for corporate clients, Ronni was ideally situated to see the potential. A feature common to all the events she managed was food. The bigger the budget, the bigger the spend on catering—and often the bigger the waste of food at the end of the night.

Ronni thought there had to be a way to bring this abundance of untouched food to those who went without. But unlike many who experience a light bulb moment, she didn't bring together a group of mates and launch the next day; she did her due diligence. Not wanting to risk duplicating what others of the 600 000 NFPs in Australia were doing, she researched the need, options and who she could partner with. No one in Australia, as far as she could discover, was operating a model similar to the one she had in her head. What she did find was an organisation doing similar things in the US, so that's where she headed next. She was determined to learn from those who were doing what she wanted to do, to discover what she could duplicate and how she could create her own for-purpose model here in Australia.

One of the things I love about OzHarvest is the clarity Ronni brings to the role it performs and to the growth of the organisation. As she clearly articulates, OzHarvest operates under four pillars:

- **Food rescue.** Wasted food is collected and distributed to those who most need it.

- **Environment.** Good food worth between $8 and $10 billion is wasted in Australia every year, millions of tonnes going straight to landfill. Keeping it out of landfill directly benefits the environment.

- **Education.** OzHarvest teaches vulnerable people how to purchase and prepare good food on a very limited budget, how to eat better and how to maximise the impact of good food on their lives.

- **Community engagement.** OzHarvest seeks to inspire, connect and create opportunities for those in the community looking to get involved but without the capacity, desire or commitment to start their own organisation. The charity is creating a pipeline for volunteers to connect more deeply with their community and to feed their souls at the same time.

It's the fourth pillar that attracted to me to OzHarvest. Ronni says, 'Community engagement is so important for the emotional health of our country. Creating an opportunity for people to give back and to do good for others is hugely important. It is about a civil society and I believe it is the way a society is measured'.

Community engagement is a key to OzHarvest's success. The organisation depends on volunteers and provides meaningful opportunities to more than 100 people every month. Part of this is creating gainful engagement that allows the volunteers to see the difference they are making, have that shared experience and feel good about themselves at the same time. The experience starts when the volunteers collect the food and develop an appreciation of the waste that would occur but for their work. Their experience is deepened when they then get to deliver the food and see the change it brings to those receiving it.

Right there is the magic, the reason why I chose to feature OzHarvest. It's not because of the great work it is doing and the number of lives it is changing among those who consume the food, but because of the number of lives it is changing among those who deliver it. An outsider could measure its success based on the number of meals it provides to those who might otherwise go hungry, or in the tonnes of landfill avoided, or in the delivery of the education programs it runs. But that would be to miss a great part of the success of what it does and who it serves.

Ronni describes the meaningful experiences provided for the volunteers as the 'very core' of their success. It's why the corporates they engage with stay with them. 'Our corporate partners support us in a number of ways, one of which is the provision of their staff, who come along and have an amazing experience and they love us. In turn they go back to work and love their employers a little more, who complete the circle by loving us even more.' It is to the experiences that bring a deeper level of engagement that Ronni attributes much of their success.

It is a great example of how a corporate and a charity can work together to create shared value for one another. That's the very essence of *doing good by doing good*.

Humpty Dumpty Foundation

The Humpty Dumpty Foundation is an Australian charity founded by Paul Francis OAM, who remains the executive chairman. The original purpose of Humpty was to support the pediatric ward at Royal North Shore Hospital in Sydney. Since Paul first set about helping sick kids in 1990, the reach of Humpty Dumpty has grown from one ward in one Sydney-based hospital to more than 214 hospitals across Australia, impacting on tens of thousands of families along the way. It has also recently started supporting a hospital in East Timor.

What it does is life-changing and without a shadow of a doubt life-saving. It stops children from dying. Listening to Paul talk about the origins, the success, and the stories of the kids and how it interacts with its supporters, you begin to understand how this humble, quiet-spoken man has led the organisation over the past twenty-odd years with controlled passion, a vision and deep resolve. Few appreciate the challenges of balancing the competing demands of maintaining a business career and a family while running an active charity; fewer still manage to do all three successfully for over a quarter of a century.

The foundation owes its success to the simplicity of its focus. For Paul and his team it is very clear that it's all about giving their supporters an outcome. It is a classic example of satisfying the 'but for' test I have spoken about throughout the book. Paul can walk a team of supporters through a hospital and point to the equipment in the theatre, emergency room or wards that sustains the most vulnerable children. He can point to equipment displaying the 'Donated by Humpty Dumpty' stickers and say, 'Without your donation and commitment, this little fella in the bed here would not be alive today'. I'm not sure there are too many experiences more powerful than that.

And there's no need to break it down and explain how much of the donation will go towards one place or another. They don't talk about improving the survival rate of sick or injured children across the country. They remove the complexity, telling their donors, 'Here is a list of equipment that is needed in these hospitals across the country. If you would like to purchase a piece of equipment we would love your support. You choose the value of your contribution and you choose the hospital you would like to support'.

Requests for equipment come to the Humpty Dumpty Foundation from the 214 hospitals it supports across the country. Each request is submitted to a task force of appropriately qualified people, who make recommendations on what the foundation should support and what it should not. The task force must be satisfied that the equipment is not going to sit in a corner and never be used and that the equipment is appropriate to the operational level of the hospital. Once the task force submits its recommendations, Paul and his team put each request into language that can be understood by non-medical people: this is why it is needed and this is what it is going to do. The list of equipment needed is then collated and put before the sponsors or donors, who are then invited to purchase a piece of equipment for a hospital of their choice to the value they choose, with a commitment that the hospital will receive it within 12 weeks. The final decision rests with the individual donor. At the end of the night, when they leave the function at which the invitation is presented, they can go home and tell their kids what change will occur because of their support. A powerful position.

Paul admits that when he started with this model of offering to 'sell' the equipment at fundraising functions he was not filled with confidence it would be successful; in fact, he feared the strategy would fail miserably. He needn't have worried. At his first attempt he raised $30 000 and all the equipment was purchased within minutes. Today Humpty raises upwards of half a million dollars at its events using the same strategy. With that kind of success why would you change.

Changing a model that works is always risky. Paul's decision to start supporting hospitals more than 30 minutes' drive from Sydney's North Shore was a leap in the dark. All of his supporters in the early days were located in a small catchment area on the North Shore, and what brought them together was tennis. When requests for support came from the Children's Hospital at Randwick and then Westmead, he was nervous as to how this would be received. The donors were now being asked to consider supporting a hospital that in all likelihood they personally would never visit or need to call upon. Paul could have put forward an argument for why it was necessary or explained how the foundation planned to expand, or even just started distributing the money raised across the hospitals. Instead he simply gave them the option of supporting at the level and location of their choice. His faith in them was confirmed as they eagerly dug deep to support all the hospitals, not just those they might one day need themselves.

The East Timor decision followed the same pattern. The option was put to 200 of its supporters: 'Should Humpty Dumpty support a hospital in East Timor?' The result: 199 voted for and just 1 against. Power rested with the donors to choose who they would support.

When I ask Paul and his general manager, Angela Garniss, why they think it is such a success, they respond in unison: 'It's the experience!' I can see the pride Paul feels when, leaning forward in his chair, he shares the following story.

'We had a donor who had spent $21 000 to purchase a laryngoscope for Royal North Shore Hospital. A three-year-old little fella by the name of Lachlan had been taken to the hospital. All of the equipment on hand and the experience of the medical team were put into saving this little boy, but it wasn't working. They couldn't remove the blockage from his throat. They had recently received the laryngoscope from our foundation, but there was a reluctance to use it as it was so new. Confidence wasn't high due to their unfamiliarity with the equipment, but the options for saving Lachlan's life were fast diminishing—other than using the laryngoscope. Such was the uniqueness of the procedure that it was recorded on video for training purposes. It was successful and they did save Lachie's life.

'What we know very clearly is if they hadn't had the laryngoscope Lachie would not be alive today. We were then able to play the video at our next fundraising event to show the difference it had made. Better than that, we had the medical team who used it to save Lachlan's life and we had Lachlan's parents at the same event to celebrate the success. You can imagine how the donor who had purchased the equipment felt when he got to meet the medical team and Lachie's parents. This is an example of the shared experience that we are able to create.'

When Paul started putting on fundraising dinners, many of his friends said, 'I'll give you $100 rather than come to your dinner'. Paul had been around the block too many times to let that be the outcome. 'Get them to the dinner and the $100 they were going to spend quickly turns into $2000.' In Paul's experience, too many charities think because they are a charity they can get away with serving potential donors a low-quality meal or cheap wine. Paul is clear that if he wants to attract corporates and expects them to bring along their clients, it needs to be a memorable night, an experience that gives them a great night out, and that includes good food and exceptional wine.

What value do his donors and corporate partners take from their relationship with Humpty Dumpty? Paul answers the question by recalling the words of one of his donors: 'You taught me how good it feels to give.' The team at Humpty sees the sense of purpose that grows within a company when it gets behind a project and can see for itself the outcomes that are a direct result of the giving. 'We create the opportunity for people to give and then we see the benefits they get from that giving. Sadly, too many people miss out on the pleasure of giving.'

From the moment I met Paul and Angela it was clear to me that they are doing remarkable work and that many families across Australia today are complete thanks to them. That is obvious very quickly. But what is equally clear is the value they attach to the experience they offer their donors and supporters. Paul speaks about the end result, saving children's lives, by telling stories. The foundation is about connecting their donors to an outcome. From the choice of wines served at their functions to personal tours through hospital wards with their donors, he is convinced that the way to success for Humpty Dumpty is to create shared experiences. Do it effectively and the task of saving lives can be left in the skilled hands of the medical teams across the country.

> 'We create the opportunity for people to give and then we see the benefits they get from that giving. Sadly, too many people miss out on the pleasure of giving.'

* * *

In the previous pages we have discussed the experiences of bike rides in Thailand, of feeding the hungry and of providing medical care for children in our hospitals. These three charities are profiled because they do experiences well. In emphasising the value of shared experiences for the participants and the charities, there is a tendency to focus on the event itself. If we focus solely on the shared experiences that each of the charities offers, however, we risk missing the bigger picture. We need to consider the relationship above and beyond the actual experience.

The relationship is what brings the two together in an enduring way. The memories of shared experiences—the hard days on the bike, the smiling faces of the children and the many hilarious moments on the road — don't end when the riders climb off their bikes for the last time. The memories and experiences live on. But what do we do with those supporters who have committed so much of themselves over a 12-month period or the sponsors who have purchased the life-saving medical equipment? The dance doesn't have to be over when the music stops.

After many years of running a charity, I know there is a tendency to finish one major event, such as the bike rides in January, draw breath and take a couple of weeks off before starting again, moving on to the next event. But could we do something more to extend the experience and keep the relationship alive well after the wheels have stopped turning? My feeling is yes we could, and we absolutely should.

How do you extend the experience you have created to provide added value to your participants, sponsors or donors? Exploring the success of the charities I have featured in this book, what emerges clearly are both the consistencies and the simplicity of the models. That's not to say the operations are simple and without immense challenges. To suggest that would indeed be to deny many of their triumphs. The simplicity is in the translation of what they do and how people can make a difference. The progressive charities and those who do social value well can best articulate it through storytelling.

When it comes to clarity in measuring input and outcomes, TOMS offers one of the simplest and therefore one of the best models. *One for one.* Three words describe how it converts its charity dollars into doing good. As a supporter you understand what you need to do to produce a given outcome in a developing country.

The progressive charities and those who do social value well can best articulate it through storytelling.

OzHarvest has a very clear message: 'For every dollar we receive we can deliver two meals to someone in need.' That is really powerful stuff and is a compelling argument when you are sitting in front of potential donors, corporate partners or even your most loyal supporters. If you have the clarity, can satisfy the 'but for' test and have transparency, then that will massively boost your credibility and trustworthiness.

Humpty Dumpty can't offer quite the same simple formula, but what it can do on a much higher level is connect donors to sick, sometimes terminally ill children through telling powerful stories of how children's lives are saved. There can be few better examples of satisfying the 'but for' test than telling a donor, 'Tonight you have purchased this piece of equipment, without which children have died in the past'. As with TOMS and OzHarvest, the basic model is simple, with a direct correlation between the donation and the difference made. Again, no messy formulas and totally believable—and the advantage of being able to tell corporate partners the story, or better still take them on a tour of the hospital.

> If you have the clarity, can satisfy the 'but for' test and have transparency, then that will massively boost your credibility and trustworthiness.

When you are making incremental improvements to a community, and projects run into the hundreds of thousands of dollars, the challenge of finding the 'one for one' increases. At Hands we are able to break down the cost of caring for each of the several hundred children across our multiple homes; we can identify the costs per child for food, education and so on. But what we have found most successful is providing very clear fundraising targets for each of our riders (the main source of our income). If the riders are participating on a corporate ride of five days, they raise $5000; if they join one of our longer rides, they raise $10 000. The figure is not negotiable, it's not a target to get close to. The rider who doesn't reach the $10 000 target doesn't ride.

The Hands model involves a very different level of engagement from buying a pair of shoes as a contribution. Both, however, make it very clear to the potential supporter what they need to do and where their contribution will go. Supporters will always look to engage on different levels. We see that at Hands, where some supporters may choose to visit one of our centres but that is the sum total of their support, while some riders return year after year, raising another $10000 each time. The charities that continue to grow are those that have found a successful way of engaging with their supporters. The sponsored bike ride model won't be for everyone; buying a pair of TOMS shoes may or may not feed your soul. The key is to find your place in the market and create a unique experience.

When I am working with other charities or talking with corporate teams about building engagement through shared experiences, I list my five experience essentials:

1 Start with the question 'How can I add value?'.

2 Be clear why you are doing it.

3 Believe in it or don't do it.

4 Become known for it.

5 Ask, 'Does it feed my soul?'.

Let me explore these in a bit more detail.

1 **Start with the question 'How can I add value?'.** At Hands when we are looking to engage with a new partner, or even when we are sending out a monthly newsletter, one question I ensure we ask is 'How are we adding value in this exchange?'. My view is that if we are talking with sponsors around an exchange of money, and that is the sum total of the conversation, I have not done my job effectively and the connection is likely to be limited. In everything we do we need to start from the place of knowing how we are going to add value to the experience. What will create the best environment for the supporter, donor or visitor to our centre so they will want to return and deepen their level of engagement?

2 **Be clear why you are doing it.** It seems pretty straightforward, but what is the purpose behind the experience you are creating? What is it you want to walk away with, and what is it you want those involved in the experience to walk away with? Once you are really clear on why you are doing it, then you can build a framework to maximise the opportunity. As a charity, do you want high participation rates, heavy exposure, low overheads or

Value of shared experiences

major fundraising as your biggest outcome? You can't have them all, so choose your most desired outcome and put your efforts into making that a success.

3   **Believe in it or don't do it**. Creating those experiences that are really meaningful and have the power to change lives, both of the recipients and of the participants, can and often does take massive amounts of time and resources from an organisation to be successful. To continue to invest these resources the team needs to believe in the purpose and the vision. Without belief and authenticity true potential won't be realised.

4   **Become known for it**. An easy measure of success of the experience you are creating is when you become known for this as much as for the core business. Many of our corporate riders sign up for the first-hand experience and engagement. The outcome of bringing change to the lives of the kids in Thailand is almost secondary. For a good number of our supporters both in Australia and internationally, Hands is mainly about the rides. This in no way detracts from what we are doing on the ground; quite the reverse, it enhances what we are able to achieve. Get the experience right and the money will come.

5   **Ask, 'Does it feed my soul?'**. This is closely connected to point 3, but it takes it to a deeper and more meaningful level. If you can achieve this then everything else becomes so much easier. For me on a personal level, riding 1600 kilometres every January with the people that come and join us is food for my soul. I get to experience the ride with those I love most in my life, and we bring amazing success to the charity. I get to witness the personal journey of the riders, and it is a privilege to be part of something that is so meaningful. The ride changes lives and provides food for the soul for many who otherwise find themselves caught on the hamster wheel of life.

The three charities profiled in this chapter were built on very different models yet share certain fundamental principles and indeed strengths:

- *The simplicity of their operational model.* Hands and Humpty both have an incredibly lean team to support the work being done. Between them they have no more than half a dozen staff yet they are raising close to $10 million per year. Given the nature of its operations, OzHarvest has a much larger team, but it too bases its work on a simple model.

- *The opportunity for engagement with their donors and corporate partners.* Each charity is very clear that the success of all they do pivots on the engagement opportunities. OzHarvest's corporate partners get a chance not only to feed those in need but, importantly, to feed their own souls at the same time. Humpty invites donors to walk through the hospitals and meet the children they are helping and their parents. Hands welcomes donors to visit any of their centres.

- *The strength of shared experiences.* For Hands it is the bike rides that change lives, particularly the riders'. Often people engage with Hands and participate in a bike ride without *really* understanding the work we do. Humpty traces the success of what it does back to the quality of the wine served at its functions. OzHarvest supporters see the food that is wasted and then see those who benefit.

- *A high level of transparency.* The results are there to see. Whether it's saving the lives of children in Australia or Thailand or providing food to those in need, the outcomes are very tangible.

- *Continuing active involvement of the founders.* In all three organisations the prime movers remain actively engaged, every day, and are accessible to those they work with and those who support their dreams.

chapter 12

SELECTING A CHARITY PARTNER

Decisions around selecting a charity partner are faced by those entering the wonderful world of CSR for the first time as well as by advanced organisations who are looking to add a new charity partner or replace an existing one. There are several ways that a potential charity partner is likely to appear on the radar:

- An 'experience' may bring it to front of mind. This may be on the back of work it is doing or an interaction by a staff member, or its work may come up for some other reason, planting the suggestion that it might be a worthy partner.

- The business will invite charities to join them in partnership for a particular cause. (This is the approach often taken by Optus on its larger projects.)

- The charity approaches the business directly with a partnership proposal on a specific project.

I find through my consulting work that selecting their charity partner is often the first thing the groups I work with want to do. They will bring together a new committee or foundation team to oversee implementation of this new and often exciting initiative. The committee will come to the first meeting looking to put forward their charity partners and hoping to leave that meeting with fundraising initiatives underway. Surely giving away money can't be hard, right?

Selecting a charity partner can be a very emotional experience for those with a personal interest. The work of the committee or the board is to remove the emotion and implement a decision-making framework that will ensure the selection of charity partners is based on a set of guiding principles rather than being carried by the most vocal or emotional team member at the meeting.

Your choice of charity partners has to make sense, and often that means it's best to check the emotion at the door. Let me share with you a personal experience that is sadly not uncommon.

I was contracted to speak about leadership on Hayman Island for a pharmaceutical company that specialises in cancer treatment. In all my presentations I speak about Hands and the lessons I have learned from building it and from those I have worked with. The client who engaged me for the conference knew about my work with Hands and also knew I would share stories from it. The evening before, over a glass of very nice champagne, he informed me that unfortunately his company would not be able to support Hands in the future as they had already chosen their charity partner. To me this was an unnecessary conversation, as I had no contrary expectation. I was there to speak about leadership, not to solicit new sponsors for Hands.

> Your choice of charity partners has to make sense, and often that means it's best to check the emotion at the door.

I presented at the conference the next day and the stories and lessons were received with great enthusiasm by all, particularly the senior leadership team. At dinner that evening the CEO announced to rapturous applause that Hands would be their charity of choice for the following year. Naturally, given the conversation the previous evening, I was surprised.

But the enthusiasm seemed to be lost somewhere between the beaches of Hayman Island and the mainland. After returning to Sydney I was to never to hear another word around their commitment, despite my repeated follow-up.

What I took from this was that they were caught up in the emotion of the stories in my keynote and allowed that to override the logic behind their choice of charity partner. Back at the office of course it made sense that their charity partner worked within the field of cancer research. The point to this story is the importance of reaching this decision only when the emotion has been stripped away.

How, then, does sentiment apply in the case of Narta, the buying group representing electrical retailers and suppliers, and their support of an Australian charity building homes for children in Thailand? The difference with Narta is it was working with a very diverse range of members so there was no obvious charity sector it 'should' be supporting. It was therefore able to build its own story through investment and early engagement. Its choice of charity partner made sense because of this engagement.

Getting the charity partner right is about defining the types of people and relationships you want. To do that you need to be clear on your values, what is most important to you, and what are the negotiables and non-negotiables for your charity partner. Developing your guiding principles allows you to make smart choices around your charity partners and also positions you well to explain to internal and external partners the choices made.

> Getting the charity partner right is about defining the types of people and relationships you want.

One of the hardest decisions the foundation committee will make is turning away a worthy cause. On the face of it, you would accept that the vast majority of charities are set up with the best intentions by committed and caring people, and that the work they do in their own space is providing a better life for someone or something. If you allow yourself to say yes based on the need or worthiness of the charity, you'd best have a very, very large pool of money and make very, very small donations, because you will be setting yourself up to support everyone. Of course that is not feasible, but to be able to say yes to a few and no to many you need a set of principles or guidelines, or a decision-making framework.

The guiding principles

Here are some guiding principles you might consider when looking to engage with a charity partner:

Charity must be a deductible gift recipient (DGR)

DGR status is awarded by the Australian Taxation Office and follows a rigorous assessment of the applying charity. Qualifying as a DGR allows donations to be tax deductible and indicates a charity has demonstrated a level of governance and compliance required by the ATO.

If this requirement is accepted by the committee as a prerequisite, it offers a degree of comfort in the charity's operations, past history and reporting to regulatory bodies. Imposing this requirement on the committee can be a double-edged sword, though. While it offers a degree of credibility and guarantees an acceptable track record, it also excludes start-up charities that are often most in need of assistance, as few of them will be DGRs. Often a corporate partner can enter a relationship with a start-up charity, helping in its formation and very much being part of its development, rather than simply donating money to an organisation that's already pretty fixed in its operations.

The obvious benefit to ensuring that charity partners are DGRs is that donations to them are tax deductible. There is a trade-off here between risk tolerance and what change you're hoping to bring about.

Location of the charity

The larger corporates will often apply this filter to ensure that funds raised by the staff and or company remain within the country in which they operate. At Hands the money is directed to the facilities we are building and running offshore; I have encountered this filter quite often, but I have also seen big companies decide they can sometimes make an exception to the general rule. We have benefited to the tune of several hundred thousand dollars in one-off donations from companies who, prior to my keynote presentation, made it clear they couldn't support us, only to turn around an hour later and offer up six-figure donations.

This is a principle I come across often but have never really been able to wrap my head around the logic behind it, other than its use as a filter. We often hear the maxim *charity begins at home*, but shouldn't we support those in greatest need, regardless of geographical boundaries?

One of the best ways around this is for a company to consider entering charity partnerships at local, national and international levels. I have seen this work effectively. It offers diversity in charity partners, opportunities for engagement and shared experiences, as well as rich relationships and possible cross-pollination.

Access to audited annual financial accounts

Under the Corporations Law companies and other legal entities are required to submit their annual accounts to ASIC. Charities are under no such statutory restrictions.

Access to such accounts, however, allows potential supporters to assess the level of spend the charity makes on the administration of its organisation and the remuneration paid to its staff. Making this an essential guiding principle allows the board to assess the reporting, income and expenditure of the charity and, to an extent, the level of governance and compliance that exists. This condition alone does not dictate the split between funds spent on project and administration costs; it merely requires access to such information.

A number of very large and well-known Australian charities hold their annual accounts close to their chest, which makes them quite hard to access. The question that immediately arises is what are they hiding? It leads you to assume one of two things is occurring. Either they have a large income base with an equally large amount of funds held in reserve, or they feel disclosure of their spend on fundraising, administration or remuneration would put off potential donors.

When the board is considering making an investment using funds that could otherwise be allocated to staff or shareholders, it needs to arrive at a decision with its eyes wide open. If you were entering a financial partnership with another entity and attaching your brand to theirs, would you be happy to do so without access to key information? I suggest that would be highly unlikely. So why risk hitching your horse to a charity wagon whose financial fitness is kept hidden?

Get clear on the charity's business and/or strategic plan

The sophistication of the business and/or strategic plan will depend on the size of the charity. Ideally, the charity you are looking to support will have a clear vision of where it is heading and how it is going to get there. It should be able to articulate its values and what it is looking to achieve over the coming three to five years.

It should also be clear on who it wants to partner with and what conditions it has in place to protect the brand image of those who are signing on to support it. What policy and procedures does the charity have in place to ensure its sponsors are not compromised. The due diligence undertaken by the business looking to partner with the charity will depend on the size of the investment and their proximity.

Percentage of funds spent by a charity partner on administration and fundraising

This guiding principle follows on from the level of transparency that the charity partner offers. Any claims by the charity partner on its level of spend should be supported by independently audited financial records. This is a topic in the charity space that you can argue with virtue on either side of the fence. Dan Pallotta makes a case for charities spending a decent proportion of their funds on administration to 'grow the pie' and argues that they actually do a disservice to those they mean to help by not doing so. But there is a generally accepted threshold, and Dan discusses how in the view of his supporters he crossed that line with the result that they withdrew his funding, ending a previously successful campaign that had raised millions of dollars.

The bigger the charity becomes, the harder it is to operate in a manner that relies on volunteers, gifts and the goodwill of the supporters, unless of course the charity can find a model to cover those expenses without spending donors' money on administration or fundraising.

Operating models and percentages of donations spent on administration are subject to a wide range of variables. The board may choose to apply what it considers an acceptable ratio between the funds reaching the charity's recipients and its expenditure on administration, fundraising and remuneration of its staff. The split may be 80:20 (with 20 per cent spent on administration) or it may be a more flexible 70:30. To cover a unique set of circumstances, a caveat of 'unless otherwise agreed by the board' might be attached. Of greater importance than the charity's claim on its spend, I would suggest, is evidence to justify the position, which will be contained in the financial records as outlined in the previous section 'Access to audited annual financial accounts'.

The charity has in place a sound board of directors

Evidence of a sound board of directors will contribute significantly to the foundation committee's confidence in the operation of the charity. In the assessment of the charity board, the committee may consider the number of directors, the tenure of the board, the frequency of changeover of members and the appropriate skill levels represented.

When a charity is starting out the board is often little more than a collection of friends and colleagues who are committed to the same cause. Many, if not most, of them would never sit on a corporate board drawing remuneration. That is not to say they are not worthy of a position on the charity board, but often their skills and exposure to governance at board level will be limited. As a charity's momentum grows, as the income and projects increase, the charity becomes more attractive to more experienced and desirable directors. Greater caution should then be taken in the assessment of prospective board members, the skill level being commensurate with the size of the organisation.

Holding a position on a charity board is desirable for a number of groups, including those who have the skills and are looking to contribute in the best way they can, and those who lack skills and look to the charity sector to fill the void as they seek paid directorships. Charities should treat the second group with caution when building their board.

When selecting a charity partner, due diligence should include conducting background checks on each of the directors of the charity board to improve your level of confidence in your prospective partners.

Allocation of funds to a specific project

The foundation committee may decide to support measurable and identifiable projects rather than contributing to general operating costs. The benefit of this is it allows the committee to measure and then report on the difference made in a clearer way than with a general donation. This is the model that works so effectively for the Humpty Dumpty Foundation. Its fundraising is targeted towards those looking to have that real, specific outcome attached to their donation.

> Its fundraising is targeted towards those looking to have that real, specific outcome attached to their donation.

This principle is difficult to apply to support research-type charities, for which it may be a 'nice to have' rather than an essential.

Opportunity to engage with the charity partner

In considering charity partners, the foundation committee may seek first to identify opportunities for members of the business to share in experiences and deepen their level of engagement, thus providing ongoing and mutual benefits. Part of the initial assessment may be to consider the mutual flow of benefits, which shouldn't be seen as flowing in one direction only.

Some charities build their events around participation, which serves to raise funds and increase awareness of their work. Others prefer to have skilled specialists perform the roles and limit engagement to fundraising. Again, the importance of this principle will depend on the desired relationship and outcomes and the values of both organisations.

Term of commitment/review

There is a standard formula for developing deep and meaningful relationships of this nature: support fewer over a longer period of time to maximise the return to all parties. It's hard to build strong relationships if the support is spread across too many charity partners. The messages can become confused or lost in the noise generated and the effectiveness is often diluted. Stability, and building on the shared strategy, offers benefits to both parties.

> Stability, and building on the shared strategy, offers benefits to both parties.

Committing to fewer for longer doesn't remove the need for frequent review and assessment of the relationship, however. It may be that the committee decides on a one- to two-year commitment that is reviewed annually. Or, should the relationship be mutually beneficial, the commitment may be open-ended but subject to review and assessment on the anniversary of the agreement.

Reporting back on KPIs

The committee may consider it prudent to establish a number of key performance indicators for the relationship with its charity partner and request that those KPIs are reported on annually or over another agreed time period.

These indicators may include how the funds were allocated, the change that was achieved, the number of interactions and the shared experiences. Measuring the change achieved in the charity sector can involve both soft and hard returns. Enriching the lives of sick children, making them laugh for a couple of hours—how do you measure the true worth of that? But where results are measurable, this can be hugely effective in reporting. OzHarvest does this very well. For every dollar donated, two meals can be provided to those in need. The beauty is in the simplicity.

The next step

These guiding principles will help shape the decision-making process around what charities will be considered the right fit for a business. In my experience of stepping into businesses to help them implement a CSR platform, few don't have a good idea of the charity partners they would like to work with. Often they have their charity of choice but want to formalise their relationship. Establishing a set of guiding principles helps the committee clarify what it is looking for in its charity partners, then it helps in communicating both internally and externally why a particular charity has been chosen.

The guiding principles will help you decide on the type of charity you are looking for and the minimum operating standards they should have, but there are a number of steps to consider beyond this. It's about the alignment of values. The guiding principles can help shape a somewhat clinical view — measures you can readily audit, similar to looking at the company's financial accounts. They will give you a picture but not the *full* picture. You really want to find out what its soul is like. Is it an organisation that meets your values? Is it a group of people you not only want to do business with but feel will enrich you and your team?

Consider the following:

- *Pilot program.* Before committing to a particular group for the longer term, start the relationship with a pilot program that will allow each of you to see how the other works.

- *Commitments.* Does it live up to the commitments it has made? With the best intentions it may have begun with a lot of promises. But for most the CSR partnership is not core business, and priorities can shift. As those priorities shift is the relationship still in line with what was promised?

- *Accessibility.* How accessible are the key partners of each organisation after the initial wave of excitement has passed? Have the deckchairs been moved and is that acceptable?

- *Quantity vs quality.* How many charity partners does the business have and how many business partners does the charity have? It's important to learn early on where you stand, what you can expect and what is the growth strategy of each stakeholder. Is the charity constantly looking to land the next business partner and if so how does that affect your relationship? It might be perfectly acceptable or it might not, but it's good to be clear about this early on.

When talking about CSR a relatively new corporate to enter the space is REA Group, which operates Australia's leading online property site realestate.com.au. Its engagement with the community is not new — it has been doing that quite successfully through its sponsorship of community initiatives and education of real estate agents. What is new, though, is its commitment to a CSR platform underpinned by the concept of shared value.

REA Group owns and operates the leading real estate and commercial property advertising sites in Australia. Its primary customers are real estate agents who sell or rent properties. It operates internationally in addition to within Australia, with a presence across Europe and Asia, and its websites are visited by over 11 million unique browsers each month. To make all this happen it employs more than 700 staff across its business and is an ASX-listed company. So while the general public might know its real estate websites, clearly it is much more than that.

REA Group's engagement strategy with the community sector crosses three areas: sponsorship of community events, which is part of its marketing platform, the education of real estate agents, and its CSR platform.

Its decision to enter the traditional CSR space was made in a quite untraditional way that was more akin to the strategic direction we are seeing from those leading in this area. Its approach is not one of corporate philanthropy but one of addressing a problem through innovation and a longer term, more strategic approach.

REA Group is in the main about providing technology to help people sell and buy their homes. Our home is where we retreat at the end of a busy day; it is where we build and nurture our families, a place of safety. Well, that's what it should be. The rates of domestic violence and the homelessness that results have reached alarming levels and continue to rise within Australia, as they have been doing since 2006. When looking to set its CSR direction, REA Group wanted to do something that aligned with its industry and values, and to introduce into the sector innovation that charity groups just would not get near otherwise.

Its early work in the space is looking towards alignment with national bodies who are working at the prevention stage rather than just the intervention stage. It is looking to partner with those groups who are addressing the deeper problem rather than just the impacts of violence and homelessness, and to this end its strategy is providing longer term support across a smaller number of external partners.

Its approach of 'fewer for longer' has been a consistent theme through this book among companies who are making the most impact. Jill Riseley, who oversees sustainability for REA Group, says, 'Our commitment to our partners will initially be over a three-year period with an option to extend after that. We recognise that the area we are choosing to operate in it can take several years to bring about change, but we are committed to the cause and for the long term'.

REA Group has established a number of conditions for selection of charity partners. Some are limiting, some dramatically reducing their options when it comes to charity partners, but it is committed to work with a coalition of partners to bring about the most effective change it can contribute. By working with multiple stakeholders it sees an opportunity in the multiplier effect, building capacity within the partners it works with. The key requirements of its program are as follows:

- alignment with the company purpose and values
- alignment to business strategy and operational impacts
- create a measurable and tangible societal difference
- enable the ability to provide a mix of financial, expertise and product
- a measurable return to the Group through the engagement and advocacy of its staff, customers and consumers.

In heading up the Sustainability program Jill Riseley has no doubt what REA expects. 'I see the work that we are doing in this space as equal to that of an investment area of the business, not too dissimilar from that of an investment banker. My role is to invest the resources of REA and earn them a return on that investment. It's not about *giving back*; it's not about presenting cheques, it's about making a sustained and significant difference in the area we choose to focus on, with a return to REA Group by creating tangible societal outcomes.'

Jill believes that it is both fair and equitable that the sustainability area of the business should be held to account, and that 'most organisations don't hold their community investment teams to the level of accountability they should, and by not holding them to account they are doing not only their teams but the entire industry a disservice'.

Here are the key lessons we can take from REA Group's approach:

- Commit to fewer for longer.
- Take a strategic approach, ensuring alignment between your purpose and values.
- Leverage the resources within the company to make the biggest difference in the charity sector.
- Make sustainability teams accountable for bringing a return to the business.

Sharing the pie

How many ways are you going to cut the pie, and who gets a slice?

GO BEYOND... CHARITY

AUDIT RESULTS

... LOOK INTO THE SOUL OF THE POTENTIAL PARTNER.

Once you have decided on the types of charities you want to support, how do you decide on the number? For some, one will be the right number; others will find many is the right fit. Unilever Global, representing 173000 employees, has five major charity partners. Churchill Education, with just 30 staff, supports six major charity partners and a number of smaller ones. Each organisation has found a model that is working for them right now.

A major consideration is the type of relationship and level of engagement you want. If your chosen model is currently one of corporate philanthropy without expectation of return, then perhaps you are happy to have more than one charity on board. If you are looking for deeper engagement, the model adopted by Jellis Craig, with two major charity partners, allows for that. For Kay Spencer, CEO and chair of Narta, selecting Hands Across the Water as its sole charity partner has allowed it to build a much deeper relationship and engagement.

Larger corporates have the option of operating like a foundation, inviting grant applications or supporting many projects aligned to a major theme within their overall CSR platform. Optus and Origin, whose core CSR tenets are vulnerable youth and education respectively, encourage their staff and external stakeholders to support a wide range of charities on more personal levels.

The key questions to ask when selecting the number of charity partners you wish to work with include the following:

- What level of engagement are you seeking?
- Is your support financial or in-kind?
- What are you seeking to gain from the relationship?
- How much time are you prepared to commit to the relationship?
- Is it part of your long-term strategy?

People can become quite passionate about a cause that is close to their heart. Understandably, someone who loses a parent at a young age to cancer or loses a child to a rare condition will see their cause as of the utmost importance. A traveller who returns from China after seeing bears held in cages for the extraction of their bile may want to channel their resources into eliminating that cruel practice. We can't help everyone, but with clarity we can all help someone.

Setting parameters for who or what will be supported, and the term of that support, allows you as a business to articulate your position clearly to those looking for your support.

- A set of guiding principles provides you with a useful framework when selecting possible charity partners. It will also ensure consistency to your approach and give you a baseline to communicate internally and externally on who you will partner with and why.

- Selecting charity partners can be an emotional process. Many people will have a favourite charity they would like to see supported.

- The guiding principles will allow you to conduct an audit of potential partners, but you need to go beyond the audit results and 'look into the soul' of the potential partner to ensure there is an alignment of values.

- In the selection of charity partners, the trend is away from offering up a sum of money and calling for interest among charity groups, and towards identifying a societal problem and then seeking out the most appropriate charity partners.

Afterword

Looking forward—what's on the horizon

The concept of corporate social responsibility has been around for decades; the term was first coined in 1953. The first company to publish a report on the work it was doing in this area was Ben and Jerry's in 1989. The real rise of CSR can be attributed to the response by corporations, in particular Shell, to anti-corporate activism. Initially, CSR focused on codes of conduct and business relating to care and respect for people and the environment. It was seen as mainly reactive—to mitigate poor corporate behaviour.

The changes we are seeing now involve business embracing the opportunities that are presented when addressing the needs of society. It is increasingly understood that 'doing good' is good for business. Shared value and similar models are not altogether groundbreaking. They don't represent a new dawn of capitalism, but they do offer many opportunities for business and the community to work together in partnership for mutual benefit in ways that previously were not considered viable.

In these last pages I have taken a crystal ball approach to look at current trends and forecast where they might lead—to make some predictions about what might be around the corner.

Importance of the supply chain

The supply chain is an essential element of the shared value model. Its inclusion in a company's CSR strategy is not new but I see the role it plays increasing. For companies with a sound CSR program in place already, this is the next frontier, the opportunity to consider what comes next. It means taking a broader view and being willing to look at their partners in a new light.

There have been a number of turning points for CSR. The Bangladesh factory collapse in April 2013 may well go down as a key event in the CSR timeline that changed companies' relationships with their partners, even those beyond their first-tier suppliers. This building collapse in the city of Dhaka claimed the lives of 1129 low-paid factory workers who were manufacturing garments for distribution throughout the Western world. The day before the disaster cracks were discovered in the building; shop workers and bank staff on the ground floor were evacuated and did not return. The factory workers were ordered back to work and threatened with the loss of a month's wages should they refuse. Just before 9 am the following day the building collapsed.

What also came out in the aftermath of the event was that these workers were being paid between $50 and $70 per month. International criticism was swift and vocal, but subsequent commitments by the manufacturers to compensate the victims' families, change working conditions and agree to binding employment standards have yet to be significantly realised.

Manufacturers can take corrective and proactive steps to right the wrongs or they can resist change, which in time will be led by the ethical base of consumers. The opportunity exists for companies to clearly articulate for their customers the 'cradle to grave' story of their products: the sources of raw materials; the working and living standards of their second- and third-tier suppliers; the wages paid to their workers; the consumption of raw materials in the manufacturing process; and what happens to the products at the end of their life (the environmental impact if they enter landfill).

> **Opportunity for business:** Show transparency in the supply chain beyond first-tier suppliers.

> **Opportunity for government:** Introduce tax incentives for manufacturers who abide by international standards of transparency and employment conditions for supply chain.

> **Opportunity for NFPs:** Take a stronger position in the advocacy of international workers and expose those companies that exploit vulnerable workers in developing countries. Equally, acknowledge those companies who perform above statutory standards.

Increase quality and frequency of reporting

Reporting in the sector is problematic for a number of reasons. There is the difficulty of trying to measure the real impact of a CSR program, the perceived value in reporting, the benchmarking standards and the voluntary nature of reporting. Simon Robinson, a director with LBG in Australia–New Zealand, believes that as few as 1 per cent of companies are currently measuring what they get out of their CSR program. If 99 per cent of companies do not truly understand the return from their CSR program, no wonder reporting and participation rates remain low. LBG claims to be 'one of the longest established and most widely used corporate responsibility standards' in the world, yet in Australia its membership sits at around 50 companies.

The reporting on environmental impacts is more advanced and evidence-based than that on the social impacts of CSR programs. As the measures for social impact become more advanced and more consistent across the business and for-purpose communities, more effective reporting will become the norm. Currently, the voluntary nature of the reporting leaves those who do decide to report great discretion in what they report on.

With increases in reporting, the data provided by groups such as LBG will become more valuable and their information richer. I anticipate a shift away from reports confined to dollars donated and volunteer time spent, towards those measuring the greater impact of the programs, both successful and unsuccessful. The 'Failure Report' produced by Engineers Without Borders is potentially more useful to both the organisation and the community than a sustainability report that focuses only on how good it is as a corporate citizen.

The *California Transparency in Supply Chains Act 2010*, which mandates reporting by businesses operating in retail or manufacture in the state of California with worldwide retail exceeding $100 million, is the first example of what will become more common legislation. Such statutes will provide customers with information they would otherwise be unable to access and will force companies to take responsibility for their supply chain partners.

Opportunity for business: Commit to measuring the impact of CSR programs, engage in reporting and benchmarking, and report on programs that were not successful as well as those that were.

Opportunity for government: Offer incentives to businesses who choose to report on CSR programs, and assist in the establishment of criteria or a reporting framework.

Opportunity for NFPs: Build capabilities for measuring the inputs, outcomes and impacts of the programs they are running with their corporate partners. Commit to providing annual impact reports on similar criteria that enable the community and corporate sectors to select charity partners based on performance.

Continued emergence of transparency-related apps and websites

An emerging trend is the growth of mobile phone applications and websites that provide consumers with information about the supply chain of the product they are considering purchasing:

- Free World is an application that allows customers to communicate with suppliers their rejection of conditions of slavery in the supply chain.

- Slavery Footprint works to engage individuals, groups and businesses in building awareness for and action against modern-day slavery.

- KnowTheChain stores reporting information on companies that are subject to the SB 657 law in the state of California.

- Global Slavery Index ranks 162 countries on a measure combining three factors: estimated prevalence of modern slavery by population, incidence of child marriage, and human trafficking in and out of the country.

- Free2Work measures brands' efforts to ensure that child and forced labour have no place in their supply chain. Grades are based on publicly available information and data self-reported by the company.

Each of the apps and websites listed here collects information, with or without the companies' active participation, and puts it into the hands of consumers. The barcode on every swing ticket or packaged item offers the manufacturer or retailer the means to share the story of the supply chain with their consumers. A web-connected mobile phone is all the consumer needs to access the information stored on the barcode. There are no technology barriers. Only corporate unwillingness can potentially stand in the way of free consumer access to this information.

Opportunity for business: Be leaders in reporting impact, giving customers the information they need to make evidence-based decisions concerning CSR-reputable companies.

Afterword

Opportunities for government: Share information gathered through various compliance and reporting measures that allow the population of these databases.

Opportunities for NFPs: Actively promote businesses who are participating in the benchmarking and align with future corporate partners who support higher levels of transparency.

Shift away from corporate philanthropy as the main component of a business's CSR strategy

As business increasingly recognises the opportunity of *doing good by doing good*, its expectations for CSR strategy will increase. Business is demonstrating a greater interest in how its dollars are used by charity partners. As we have seen, for example in the case of Optus, larger corporates are taking the lead on these social challenges and then looking to find their own charity partners. The more sophisticated CSR platforms will see less cash exchanged and a greater contribution from the programs they are supporting.

As the shift away from corporate philanthropy increases we are likely to see greater participation rates in programs that offer shared value. Business recognises the opportunities to reach new customers and enter new markets. There will be expectations of producing a positive business return from CSR, paralleling those from other business units within a corporate entity.

With increasing adoption of reporting and benchmarking, business will be better able to measure the return on investment in its CSR programs. As business better understands the benefits, particularly of shared value, its interest and investment will increase.

Opportunities for business: Move from a philanthropic to a shared value model; increasing economic returns will flow back to business.

Opportunities for government: Enter into joint-venture partnerships with both business and the NFP sector in addressing the needs of society, which would otherwise fall to government and/or the NFP sector.

Opportunities for NFPs: As the corporate and business partners of the NFP sector find greater returns through their CSR programs, they will be encouraged to expand their investment. The NFP sector can lead this discussion, particularly among its small to medium-sized business partners.

Change in the charity sector

As the level of engagement increases within the entire CSR space, businesses expect a greater return on their investment and the investment made by the for-profit sector changes, so too will the charity sector. *Doing good by doing good* can only be achieved if the for-purpose sector gets on board, recognising that what worked in the past might not necessarily be enough moving forward.

There will be opportunities for charities to do one of three things:

- Change with the market as it changes and be part of the move towards a relationship in which both sides need to benefit.

- Take a leadership role and help their current and future business partners grow through shared value.

- Remain the same and continue to rely on corporate philanthropy in what I would suggest is a diminishing, or at the very least a limiting, market, where their survival is anything but assured.

Charities will increasingly embrace the opportunities offered by a shared value model. I also foresee a commitment by charities to becoming more sophisticated and creative in their pitch for donors' money. Not only will there be an increased move towards 'experience' campaigns by charities, but I suggest there will be less appetite in the community for 'pity-style' campaigns or the 'sale of goats'. Business's desire for experiences will also see growing opportunities for small or medium-sized charities who can offer the experience sought by their corporate partners as they move away from a direct funding model.

Afterword

There will be a greater level of sophistication in the offering made by the for-purpose sector and therefore a widening of the gap between large and small charities. As the charity sector's operations become more sophisticated it is likely to attract a higher level of talent among graduates who would otherwise head straight to the corporate sector. For this to occur the mindset around remuneration will need to change to allow greater competition between the for-profit and for-purpose sectors.

Opportunities for business: A dynamic charity sector that is more aligned towards the needs of business will make for an enriching relationship.

Opportunities for government: A greater alignment between the business and NFP sectors will result in greater efficiencies and reduced demand on government services.

Opportunities for NFPs: A relationship that enriches business will result in a more rewarding and engaging relationship between the sectors. By responding to the opportunities, the NFP partners will find more resources to meet the needs they seek to address.

Increasing investment in R&D

The return on business investment in research and development into the challenges faced by society will increase. As businesses enjoy the profits of their investment they will be encouraged to renew and increase their spend. After investing $1.8 billion in R&D in new markets, GE enjoyed a return of $10 for every $1 invested—a clear incentive to continue that commitment!

Returns on R&D investment bring new markets, new customers and a refinement in operations that might otherwise have been considered unviable. Business increasingly sees society's challenges not as requiring them to donate money but rather as affording business opportunities. We will see a rise in mutually beneficial joint-venture relationships as businesses leverage their resources at the same time as they leverage the expertise that sits within the NFP sector.

Opportunities for business: With an increase in the return on R&D investment, business finds new markets, new customers and new opportunities.

Opportunities for government: By embarking on joint-venture partnerships with business, governments enjoy the benefits of meeting society's needs and reducing their spend on social welfare–type support.

Opportunities for NFPs: The NFP sector enjoys the benefits of investment in corporate R&D, discovering new solutions to problems that were previously theirs alone to solve.

Afterword

Index

'CSR' stands for corporate social responsibility

Guy Downes is an illustrator who helps individuals and organisations connect with the audiences that matter to them using a range of visual techniques such as illustration, doodles, cartoons, graphic recording, journey maps and video scribing.

With many people's preference being for visual learning, Guy's expertise can help capture attention, quicken understanding, drive engagement and spark conversation and thinking.

For more information on Guy and his work, please visit: www.guydownes.com.au

Learn more with practical advice from our experts

Above the Line
Michael Henderson

The One Thing to Win at the Game of Business
Creel Price

First Be Nimble
Graham Winter

Lead with Wisdom
Mark Strom

Stop Playing Safe
Margie Warrell

Who Killed Creativity
Andrew Grant and Gaia Grant, with Jason Gallate

Hooked
Gabrielle Dolan and Yamini Naidu

The New Rules of Management
Peter Cook

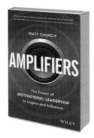

Amplifiers
Matt Church